God's Presence, God's Power in His Word and in Prayer

Watch and Pray
Matthew 26:41

(A Commentary Study in Matthew Part III &
The Promises of God and Daily Devotions)

Dr. Dorothy Batts

No portion of this book may be reproduced in any form without the expressed written consent of the author or publisher. All rights reserved.

Permission forms are available by calling our administrative office Monday-Thursday from 10:00 a.m. to 12:00 noon at (910) 423-2999. Information will be sent to you free of charge.

God's Presence, God's Power in His Word and in Prayer
Watch and Pray
Matthew 26:41
(A Commentary Study in Matthew Part III & The Promises of God and Daily Devotions)

Copyright © 2014 by Dr. Dorothy Batts
ISBN: 978-0-9914246-7-2
First Edition
Printed in the United States of America

All scriptures taken from the King James Version of the Holy Bible

2 4 6 8 10 9 7 5 3 1

Cover design & layout by Bryan K. Reed - braynkreed.com
Edited by D. Renee Gibbs

Published by
Cranberry Quill Publishing, Inc.
111 Lamon Street, Suite 204, Fayetteville, NC 28301
www.CranberryQuill.com

Table Of Contents

1	Watch And Pray God's Promises
9	God's Promises
11	God's Promises Over Fear
11	God's Promises For Senior Citizens
13	Matthew Chapter Twenty-One
17	Matthew Chapter Twenty-One - The Lord Hath Need Of Them
23	Matthew Chapter Twenty-One - Questions For Application
25	Matthew Chapter Twenty-Two
27	Matthew Chapter Twenty-Two - Love The Lord Thy God
30	Matthew Chapter Twenty-Two - Questions For Application
33	Matthew Chapter Twenty-Three
35	Matthew Chapter Twenty-Three - Blessed Is He That Cometh In The Name Of The Lord
37	Matthew Chapter Twenty-Three - Questions For Application
39	Matthew Chapter Twenty-Four
43	Matthew Chapter Twenty-Four - What Shall Be The Sign Of His Coming?
47	Matthew Chapter Twenty-Four - Questions For Application
49	Matthew Chapter Twenty-Five
51	Matthew Chapter Twenty-Five - Come, Ye Blessed Of My Father
55	Matthew Chapter Twenty-Five - Questions For Application
57	Matthew Chapter Twenty-Six
61	Matthew Chapter Twenty-Six - Watch And Pray That Ye Enter Not Into Temptation
65	Matthew Chapter Twenty-Six - Questions For Application
67	Matthew Chapter Twenty-Seven
71	Matthew Chapter Twenty-Seven - Thou Sayest
73	Matthew Chapter Twenty-Seven - Questions For Application
75	Matthew Chapter Twenty-Eight
77	Matthew Chapter Twenty-Eight - Fear Not Ye: For I Know That Ye Seek Jesus
79	Matthew Chapter Twenty-Eight - Questions For Application
81	Concluding Thought - Come Boldly

GOD'S PRESENCE IN PRAYER

"These things I have spoken unto you, that in me ye might have peace. In the world ye shall have tribulation: but be of good cheer; I have overcome the world."
John 16:33

We are living in the last days. Those who are positioned in Christ Jesus, who is the Living and Powerful Word of God, do not have anything to worry about. Jesus has commanded you to have peace for you have been translated out of the kingdom of darkness into the kingdom of God.

In the kingdom is the presence of God as you pray and have faith in the Word of God. As you study each chapter of God's Word contained in this book, your faith is being added to and your joy is being full. As you obey the Word of God you know, you are lifting Jesus up and Jesus will draw all men unto Himself.

Many will be drawn out of a world of tribulation and receive the joy of the Lord. There is hope, joy, peace and power in the Word of God.

WATCH AND PRAY GOD'S PROMISES

"Watch and pray, that ye enter not into temptation: the spirit indeed is willing, but the flesh is weak."
Matthew 26:41

In Matthew chapter twenty-six, Jesus is praying for us as He also prays for Himself. There is power when we pray. His first prayer in verses 36-38 was for every child of God to have victory over the sorrows of life the devil would send their way. Jesus, the Son of God; Emmanuel (God with us), was already endowed with power to overcome sorrow. But when He took on flesh to suffer for us, He also took on the pain of suffering.

That word "sorrow" from my own definition is "the weight, presser and pain pressing you beyond your measure of endurance until you feel your power to prevail is gone." On the other hand, Webster defines "sorrow" as "mental suffering caused by loss, disappointment and grief." Only Jesus can bring deliverance to your mind. Only Jesus can bring deliverance to your spirit, soul and body.

It was this "exceeding sorrowful prayer" that Jesus prayed for us before the enemy came, that always causes us to triumph. When sickness comes upon your body and the doctors give it a name, you must have faith in God's Word. I received my Doctoral in Theology. I am not a medical doctor, but I do believe God has raised up spirit-filled Christian doctors with wisdom to help us finish our earthly assignment with victory, peace and the power of God.

When King Hezekiah became sick unto death in 2 Kings chapter 20, the Lord sent the Prophet Isaiah to diagnose his illness and administer the cure. Isaiah was a prophet serving as God's physician. The diagnosis was, "Set thine house in order; for thou shalt die, and not live." (2 Kings 20:1b)

The sickness could have been cancer, a blood disorder that caused the body to produce boils. It does not matter what name was given this sickness; the end result was death. The first thing Hezekiah did was to first seek God in prayer. To pray the prayer Hezekiah prayed, he must have been one who meditated in God's Word. Through his meditation upon God's Word, his faith had grown to the point that he could ask God to let him live a little while longer.

In 2 Kings 20:2-3, Hezekiah prayed these words…

> *"Then he turned his face to the wall, and prayed unto the LORD, saying, I beseech thee, O LORD, remember now how I have walked before thee in truth and with a perfect heart, and have done that which is good in thy sight. And Hezekiah wept sore."*

Before Isaiah could get in the court, God stopped him and sent him back to Hezekiah with these words in 2 Kings 20:5-6…

> *"Turn again, and tell Hezekiah the captain of my people, Thus saith the LORD, the God of David thy father, I have heard thy prayer, I have seen thy tears: behold, I will heal thee: on the third day thou shalt go up unto the house of the LORD. And I will add unto thy days fifteen years; and I will deliver thee and this city out of the hand of the king of Assyria; and I will defend this city for mine own sake, and for my servant David's sake."*

In 2 Kings 20:7, Isaiah the prophet became a doctor with the prescription for Hezekiah's healing. It is written…

> *"And Isaiah said, Take a lump of figs. And they took and laid it on the boil, and he recovered."*

It does not matter what your sickness is, Jesus took it upon His body and Jesus prayed for you. The Word of God is like a medicine. When you meditate upon God's Word day and night, that Word is released first in your mind to change your thinking. You must take on the mind of Christ when you have been told you have an incurable sickness.

You must meditate upon God's Word until your faith has grown to the place of being merry. The Word of God tells us in Proverbs 17:22, "A merry heart doeth good like a medicine: but a broken spirit drieth the bones."

Hezekiah did not have a merry heart until he prayed and remembered God's Word. He faced death, but he would not lose his faith and his focus on God. If you have been given a report by the doctor that you do not have but a few months or a few years to live, begin to speak God's Word over your life and into your life. Keep in mind God told us in Matthew 6:34a, "Take therefore no thought for the morrow…" I know now why God told us never to take thought for tomorrow. Tomorrow never comes. You are living in today. When tomorrow arrives, it will be today. You do not need to fear the unknown. God has promised you today.

God told Joshua in Joshua 1:8-9…

> *"This book of the law shall not depart out of thy mouth; but thou shalt meditate therein day and night, that thou mayest observe to do according to all that is written therein: for then thou shalt make thy way prosperous, and then thou shalt have good success. Have not I commanded thee? Be strong and of a good courage; be not afraid, neither be thou dismayed: for the LORD thy God is with thee whithersoever thou goest."*

You are alive today. Enjoy your life today. Anything that causes you to become exceeding sorrowful, you must have faith and believe Jesus has already prayed for you.

Hezekiah had to follow the instructions of Isaiah, who was serving as God's physician. If he had not followed the instructions of Isaiah, he could have died. It is the will of God that you live out your appointed time upon the earth one day at a time. Only God knows the time of your departure.

Due to the fall of Adam and Eve, we live in a body of death. The body is slowly dying because our bodies are control by time. We, who have received Jesus as Savior of our lives, have received eternal life. Eternal life lives inside of us. The day will come when we will take off this body of sickness and death. But until that day comes, the devil will attack the body with infirmities. It does not matter how many times he come and attack your body; Jesus prayed for you, not only once, but three times before He went to the cross.

In Psalms 34:17-19, David wrote...

> *"The righteous cry, and the LORD heareth, and delivereth them out of all their troubles. The LORD is nigh unto them that are of a broken heart; and saveth such as be of a contrite spirit. Many are the afflictions of the righteous: but the LORD delivereth him out of them all."*

It does not matter what has cause you to become exceeding sorrowful; Jesus prayed for you. The name of your sorrow and pain might have been divorce; there is healing and restoration after this. Don't blame yourself. You are not the victim; you are victorious in Christ. Your healing will come as you meditate upon the Word of God day and night. There is power to survive this pain. You are on your way to power and peace after this process.

I also speak into and over the lives of those who has had years of delay in reaching their dreams. God told me to speak over and into your life from Jeremiah 29:11-13. Most Christians are familiar with Jeremiah 29:11, but God spoke in my heart and said, "Tell My people who has become weary in their waiting and there has been years of delay in their visions and dreams; it was only a delay but not a denial." It is written in Jeremiah 29:11-13 these words...

> *"For I know the thoughts that I think toward you, saith the LORD, thoughts of peace, and not of evil, to give you an expected end. Then shall ye call upon me, and ye shall go and pray unto me, and I will hearken unto you. And ye shall seek me, and find me, when ye shall search for me with all your heart."*

The Word of God through the power of Holy Spirit and the blood of Jesus will give you the power you need to live an overcoming life until your miracle comes. In Revelation 12:11a, John wrote, "And they overcame him by the blood of the Lamb, and by the word of their testimony..."

Jesus prayed in Matthew 26:37-44 three times. The number "three" is a type and shadow of resurrection. If you must drink the cup of suffering and pain for a season, you must have faith in God that your day of resurrection will come. He will give you sufficient grace to endure until your deliverance comes, and your deliverance will come. I don't know the day or the hour, but you must remember God does not lie. He said in 2 Corinthians 1:20, "For all the promises of God in him are yea, and in him Amen, unto the glory of God by us."

"…Have faith in God." (Mark 11:22) "So then faith cometh by hearing, and hearing by the word of God." (Romans 10:17) Each chapter in this book begins with a complete chapter from the Bible. As you read each chapter, you are increasing your faith and you are renewing your mind to think like Christ.

As your faith increases, you must pray the promises of God over the situation and also into that problem believing in the power of God to change the situation. God's promises to you are "…yea, and in him Amen…" That word "Amen" means "let it be as God has decreed." I have listed several promises to help you get started. For those of you who believe God for healing, I will share with you the power of God to restore life and His grace that is keeping my husband alive.

The doctors call it "unremarkable." Every night before he goes to bed, my daughter or the caregiver read Scriptures to him. He has been battling with early signs of prostate cancer, declining heart rate, diabetes, dementia, Alzheimer and he cannot walk, talk or care for his basic needs. In 2013, he was assigned to hospice. He out-lived the expected time for him to die, so they had to release him back into our care in 2013. Praise God for the miracle!

I am also a miracle. After many years of damaging my body with junk food, fried foods and carbonated drinks (better known as sodas), my heart became weak and my joints were also affected. During noon day prayer one Wednesday, I became too weak to get up off my knees. Those who were attending prayer assisted me to the car and my daughter took me to my primary physician. My heart became too weak to pump blood throughout my body. The doctor called E.M.S and I was taken from the doctor's office to the hospital.

Late that night, I heard the nurse outside my room after she had taken my vital signs, asking the head nurse if she was getting a low heart rate on Mrs. Batts. The head nurse's reply must have been "yes." The next day when my doctor came to my room, I shared with him what I had heard. He told me they did not know why they could not get my heart rate up. Everything they had done had failed. My heart rate was still dangerously low. After I was told by the doctor everything they had done was not working, I knew my work here on earth was not completed. I told the doctor I had to be at church on that Saturday night because my Men's Ministry was having their first musical anniversary.

The doctor knew I was a pastor. He said, "Pastor Batts, I don't know how long you will be here. I plan to have a therapist to come in to teach you how to walk with a cane." I begged and pleaded with him. He did get the therapist. By faith, I walked without fainting but he did not change his mind. I cannot remember all of the details, but I must have done like Hezekiah did. I must have turned my face to the wall and cried out to God. No one knew I was in the hospital except for those who were in noon day prayer with me. I did not want my members to worry or cancel any plans. I knew I had to be there on Saturday night. It was now Thursday.

There is power in prayer and praying the promises of God. I do not know if the hospital became over crowded because it was a weekend. That Saturday night about 7:30 or 8:00, my doctor came in and said he was going to release me but I must go home, get in bed and report to him on Monday morning. I did go home by the route of my church. The place was packed and the Lord was present to heal. I had promised God I would take better care of my body if He would take care of my heart.

The Word of God tells us in Ephesians 4:27, "Neither give place to the devil." I had given place to the devil by abusing my body for many years. I was addictive to sugar, chocolate, fried foods and fried chicken was my number one meal. The second favorite was pork barbecue, white bread with margarine and white rice. I cannot forget homemade gravy with onions. I also ate late at night. After that wake-up call with a near death experience, I knew I had to make some changes in my life so that I could claim God's promises in Psalms 91:15-16 which reads…

> *"He shall call upon me, and I will answer him: I will be with him in trouble; I will deliver him, and honour him. With long life will I satisfy him, and shew him my salvation."*

I must say, I never diet. All my life I had diet with every group I knew: the low carbs, the low fat and one diet pill after another. It is not that these programs will not work; it is just that I never changed my way of thinking about food. I ate all of the wrong things and I got wrong results.

That principle applies to everything in life. You must have the right mind set. You can pray every day, read God's Word 24 hours a day, attend Bible Study and church; but keep your old way of thinking. You will continue to get the same results. My daughter came by my home one morning and said, "Mom, I have come by and I want you to walk to the corner with me." By the end of two or three months, we were walking three miles.

I purposed in my heart I would not eat fried chicken and I also stopped eating beef and pork. Bake chicken and turkey became my meats. I changed my bread to honey wheat bread. I must be honest with you, I still love french fries. So, when I do get a taste for french fries; I eat them one by one after I have taken a napkin and squeezed all of the grease out of them. As soon as I feel my taste buds have been satisfied, I'll give the remaining fries away. I do not drink carbonated drinks. 90% of my liquid consumption is water and orange juice. The other 10% is other fruit juices and occasionally, green tea. I have begun to eat brown rice and wheat bread. For my sweet tooth, I keep the 100 calories, low fat cookies and gram crackers on hand; but I just do not have the same desires for sweets I once had.
I eat a lot of fruit, vegetables and dry roasted, no salt nuts. When the

enemy attacked my body, I was almost 200 pounds and wore a size 16 and 18. Without dieting, I changed my way of thinking about food. I do not live so that I can eat everything I like; I eat so that I can live a full, abundant life for my Lord and Savior, Jesus Christ. A little over seven years later, I kept my weight around 175 to 179. I know the doctors would consider me over weight at 5 feet 4 inches, but I do not diet and I walk my stairs many times during the day. I also wear a size 12 and 14.

When I went to the cardiologist for a check-up, he asked me how I was doing. I told him, "What God and you told me to do, I have been doing it and I feel great." He examined me and he told me to set up an appointment in a year. Praise God! When my primary care physician examined me at my follow-up appointment, my blood pressure was 120/80. I can never remember having a blood pressure of 120/80. With the birth of my first child, I had toxemia. From that time on, I had suffered from hypertension and heart problems for years. God did just what He said in Jeremiah 30:17a which reads, "For I will restore health unto thee, and I will heal thee of thy wounds, saith the LORD…"

God promised us in Exodus 23:25 He would take sickness from our midst. You must believe God's Word when the enemy attacks you with sickness. It is written in Exodus 23:25, "And ye shall serve the LORD your God, and he shall bless thy bread, and thy water; and I will take sickness away from the midst of thee."

GOD'S PROMISES

"And being fully persuaded that, what he had promised, he was able also to perform."
Romans 4:21

"Whereby are given unto us exceeding great and precious promises: that by these ye might be partakers of the divine nature, having escaped the corruption that is in the world through lust."
2 Peter 1:4

"For his anger endureth but a moment; in his favour is life: weeping may endure for a night, but joy cometh in the morning."
Psalms 30:5

"Many are the afflictions of the righteous: but the LORD delivereth him out of them all."
Psalms 34:19

"The LORD will strengthen him upon the bed of languishing: thou wilt make all his bed in his sickness."
Psalms 41:3

"And call upon me in the day of trouble: I will deliver thee, and thou shalt glorify me."
Psalms 50:15

"When thou passest through the waters, I will be with thee; and through the rivers, they shall not overflow thee: when thou walkest through the fire, thou shalt not be burned; neither shall the flame kindle upon thee."
Isaiah 43:2

"For our light affliction, which is but for a moment, worketh for us a far more exceeding and eternal weight of glory;"
2 Corinthians 4:17

"And he said unto me, My grace is sufficient for thee: for my strength is made perfect in weakness. Most gladly therefore will I rather glory in my infirmities, that the power of Christ may rest upon me."
2 Corinthians 12:9

"Beloved, think it not strange concerning the fiery trial which is to try you, as though some strange thing happened unto you:" But rejoice, inasmuch as ye are partakers of Christ's sufferings; that, when his glory shall be revealed, ye may be glad also with exceeding joy."
1 Peter 4:12-13

"That it might be fulfilled which was spoken by Esaias the prophet, saying, Himself took our infirmities, and bare our sicknesses."
Matthew 8:17

"There shall not any man be able to stand before thee all the days of thy life: as I was with Moses, so I will be with thee: I will not fail thee, nor forsake thee."
Joshua 1:5

"For the promise is unto you, and to your children, and to all that are afar off, even as many as the Lord our God shall call."
Acts 2:39

"And when thy son asketh thee in time to come, saying, What mean the testimonies, and the statutes, and the judgments, which the LORD our God hath commanded you?"
Deuteronomy 6:20

"Train up a child in the way he should go: and when he is old, he will not depart from it."
Proverbs 22:6

"There is one body, and one Spirit, even as ye are called in one hope of your calling;"
Ephesians 4:4

"That they may teach the young women to be sober, to love their husbands, to love their children,"
Titus 2:4

"Only take heed to thyself, and keep thy soul diligently, lest thou forget the things which thine eyes have seen, and lest they depart from thy heart all the days of thy life: but teach them thy sons, and thy sons' sons;"
Deuteronomy 4:9

"And that their children, which have not known any thing, may hear, and learn to fear the LORD your God, as long as ye live in the land whither ye go over Jordan to possess it."
Deuteronomy 31:13

"And all thy children shall be taught of the LORD; and great shall be the peace of thy children."
Isaiah 54:13

"Lo, children are an heritage of the LORD: and the fruit of the womb is his reward."
Psalms 127:3

GOD'S PROMISES OVER FEAR

"And he said unto them, Why are ye so fearful? how is it that ye have no faith?"
Mark 4:40

"For I the LORD thy God will hold thy right hand, saying unto thee, Fear not; I will help thee."
Isaiah 41:13

"But whoso hearkeneth unto me shall dwell safely, and shall be quiet from fear of evil."
Proverbs 1:33

"Then shalt thou walk in thy way safely, and thy foot shall not stumble." When thou liest down, thou shalt not be afraid: yea, thou shalt lie down, and thy sleep shall be sweet. Be not afraid of sudden fear, neither of the desolation of the wicked, when it cometh. For the LORD shall be thy confidence, and shall keep thy foot from being taken."
Proverbs 3:23-26

GOD'S PROMISES FOR SENIOR CITIZENS

"And thine age shall be clearer than the noonday; thou shalt shine forth, thou shalt be as the morning."
Job 11:17

"The glory of young men is their strength: and the beauty of old men is the gray head." (Proverbs 20:29)
"For length of days, and long life, and peace, shall they add to thee."
Proverbs 3:2

"Ye shall observe to do therefore as the LORD your God hath commanded you: ye shall not turn aside to the right hand or to the left. Ye shall walk in all the ways which the LORD your God hath commanded you, that ye may live, and that it may be well with you, and that ye may prolong your days in the land which ye shall possess."
Deuteronomy 5:32-33

"I am as a wonder unto many; but thou art my strong refuge. Let my mouth be filled with thy praise and with thy honour all the day. Cast me not off in the time of old age; forsake me not when my strength faileth."
Psalms 71:7-9

"I will go in the strength of the Lord GOD: I will make mention of thy righteousness, even of thine only. O God, thou hast taught me from my youth: and hitherto have I declared thy wondrous works. Now also when I am old and grayheaded, O God, forsake me not; until I have shewed thy strength unto this generation, and thy power to every one that is to come."
Psalms 71:16-18

MATTHEW CHAPTER TWENTY-ONE

"And when they drew nigh unto Jerusalem, and were come to Bethphage, unto the mount of Olives, then sent Jesus two disciples, Saying unto them, Go into the village over against you, and straightway ye shall find an ass tied, and a colt with her: loose them, and bring them unto me. And if any man say ought unto you, ye shall say, The Lord hath need of them; and straightway he will send them. All this was done, that it might be fulfilled which was spoken by the prophet, saying, Tell ye the daughter of Sion, Behold, thy King cometh unto thee, meek, and sitting upon an ass, and a colt the foal of an ass. And the disciples went, and did as Jesus commanded them, And brought the ass, and the colt, and put on them their clothes, and they set him thereon. And a very great multitude spread their garments in the way; others cut down branches from the trees, and strawed them in the way. And the multitudes that went before, and that followed, cried, saying, Hosanna to the Son of David: Blessed is he that cometh in the name of the Lord; Hosanna in the highest. And when he was come into Jerusalem, all the city was moved, saying, Who is this? And the multitude said, This is Jesus the prophet of Nazareth of Galilee. And Jesus went into the temple of God, and cast out all them that sold and bought in the temple, and overthrew the tables of the moneychangers, and the seats of them that sold doves, And said unto them, It is written, My house shall be called the house of prayer; but ye have made it a den of thieves. And the blind and the lame came to him in the temple; and he healed them. And when the chief priests and scribes saw the wonderful things that he did, and the children crying in the temple, and saying, Hosanna to the Son of David; they were sore displeased, And said unto him, Hearest thou what these say? And Jesus saith unto them, Yea; have ye never read, Out of the mouth of babes and sucklings thou hast perfected praise? And he left them, and went out of the city into Bethany; and he lodged there. Now in the morning as he returned into the city, he hungered. And when he saw a fig tree in the way, he came to it, and found nothing thereon, but leaves only, and said unto it, Let no fruit grow on thee henceforward for ever. And presently the fig tree withered away. And when the disciples saw it, they marvelled, saying, How soon is the fig tree withered away! Jesus answered and said unto them, Verily I say unto you, If ye have faith, and doubt not, ye shall not only do this which is done to the fig tree, but also *if ye shall say unto this mountain, Be thou removed, and be thou cast into the sea; it shall be done. And all things, whatsoever ye shall ask in prayer, believing, ye shall receive. And when he was come into the temple, the chief priests and the elders of the people came unto him as he was teaching, and said, By what authority doest thou these things? and who gave thee this authority? And Jesus answered and said unto them, I also will ask you one thing, which if ye tell me, I in like wise will tell you by what authority I do these things. The baptism of John, whence was it? from heaven, or of men? And they reasoned with themselves, saying, If we shall say, From heaven; he will say unto us, Why did ye not then believe him? But if we shall say, Of men; we fear the people; for all hold John as a prophet. And they answered Jesus, and said, We cannot tell. And he said unto them, Neither tell I you by what authority I do these things. But what think ye? A certain man had two sons; and he came to the first, and said, Son, go work to day in my vineyard. He answered and said, I will not: but afterward he repented, and went. And he came to the second, and said likewise. And he answered and said, I go, sir: and went not. Whether of them twain did the will of his father? They say unto him, The first. Jesus saith unto them, Verily I say unto you, That the publicans and the harlots go into the kingdom of God before you. For John came unto you in the way of righteousness, and ye believed him not: but the publicans and the harlots believed him: and ye, when ye had seen it, repented not afterward, that ye might believe him. Hear another parable: There was a certain householder, which planted a vineyard, and hedged it round about, and digged a winepress in it, and built a tower, and let it out to husbandmen, and went into a far country: And when the time of the fruit drew near, he sent his servants to the husbandmen, that they might receive the fruits of it. And the husbandmen took his servants, and beat one, and killed another, and stoned another. Again, he sent other servants more than the first: and they did unto them likewise. But last of all he sent unto them his son, saying, They will reverence my son. But when the husbandmen saw the son, they said among themselves, This is the heir; come, let us kill him, and let us seize on his inheritance. And they caught him, and cast him out of the vineyard, and slew him. When the lord therefore of the vineyard cometh, what will he do unto those husbandmen? They say unto him, He will miserably destroy those wicked men, and will let out his vineyard unto other husbandmen, which shall render him the fruits in their seasons.*

Jesus saith unto them, Did ye never read in the scriptures, The stone which the builders rejected, the same is become the head of the corner: this is the Lord's doing, and it is marvellous in our eyes? Therefore say I unto you, The kingdom of God shall be taken from you, and given to a nation bringing forth the fruits thereof. And whosoever shall fall on this stone shall be broken: but on whomsoever it shall fall, it will grind him to powder. And when the chief priests and Pharisees had heard his parables, they perceived that he spake of them. But when they sought to lay hands on him, they feared the multitude, because they took him for a prophet."

MATTHEW CHAPTER TWENTY-ONE
"THE LORD HATH NEED OF THEM"

WORD OF FAITH SCRIPTURES FOR MEDITATION:

"And when they drew nigh unto Jerusalem, and were come to Bethphage, unto the mount of Olives, then sent Jesus two disciples, Saying unto them, Go into the village over against you, and straightway ye shall find an ass tied, and a colt with her: loose them, and bring them unto me. And if any man say ought unto you, ye shall say, The Lord hath need of them; and straightway he will send them."
Matthew 21:1-3

WORD OF GOD MESSAGE FOR APPLICATION

The loosing of the ass and colt, I believe, is a fulfillment of prophecy in Zechariah 9:9 and also a type and shadow of the young and old being used by Jesus once they are loosed and set free. It does not matter if you are young or old, an apostle, prophet (prophetess), evangelist, pastor or teacher; Jesus wants to use you to first loose those who have the spirit of an ass and of a colt, then bring them to Jesus.

If anyone asks you why you are loosing a family member, a friend, a co-worker, an employer, a fellow brother or sister in Christ, you are to tell them "The Lord hath need of them." There are too many in the body of Christ still tied up with anger, fear, discouragement, sickness and other attacks of the enemy and no one has loosed them and brought them to Jesus. Notice I said, "Loose them and bring them to Jesus." The apostles, prophets, evangelists, pastors and teachers are doing a great work by preaching and teaching the gospel of Jesus Christ. I thank God for you. The gospel of Jesus Christ will always loose the bonds of the wicked.

After you have loosed them, your job is not over until you have brought them to Jesus and allowed Jesus to sit upon them. Jesus Christ, who is the living Word of God; Jesus Christ, who is the Anointed One to empower and set free, sat upon them. Now, they are equipped to fulfill the need of the Lord. They are also empowered to trust, obey and follow the King.

In verses 5-6, it reads...

> "Tell ye the daughter of Sion, Behold, thy King cometh unto thee, meek, and sitting upon an ass, and a colt the foal of an ass. And the disciples went, and did as Jesus commanded them."

My question to you is, "Are you doing what Jesus has commanded you to do?" In John 8:31, Jesus said, "If ye continue in my word, then are ye my disciples indeed." (John 8:31)

Again, I ask you, "Are you doing what Jesus has asked you to do?" If you are doing what He has asked you to do, His presence will sit upon you and you will have the peace of God that only comes from His presence. When the presence of the Lord is upon you, Jesus will be honored. When Jesus is lifted up, He will draw all men unto Himself. He is lifted up through the teaching and preaching of the gospel and also through our Christ-like lives. We must love Him enough to be like He is.

"Herein is our love made perfect, that we may have boldness in the day of judgment: because as he is, so are we in this world." (1 John 4:17)

The gospel of Jesus Christ teaches us how we are to lift up Jesus through our knowledge of Him. The Apostle Paul wrote in Philippians 3:10 which read, "That I may know him, and the power of his resurrection, and the fellowship of his sufferings, being made conformable unto his death."

The power of the gospel of Jesus Christ is revealed in the cursing of the fig tree as Jesus was on His way to the city. There was a fig tree with leaves and no fruit. There were two gospel messages. I believe Jesus was not only teaching His disciples, but He was also teaching those who were going to be saved in the years to come.

(I) The First Message – Do not try to represent something you are not. The Scribes and Pharisees tried to manifest a life that was looking for Jesus, but they fail to connect themselves to Him so that they could bring forth the fruit of Him.

Jesus said in John 15:7, "If ye abide in me, and my words abide in you, ye shall ask what ye will, and it shall be done unto you."

(II) The Second Message – "… if ye shall say unto this mountain, Be thou removed, and be thou cast into the sea; it shall be done." (Matthew 21:21b)

Through the gospel of Jesus Christ and your faith in God, you will come to a place in God that you believe His Word. Also, Jesus said in Matthew 21:22, "And all things, whatsoever ye shall ask in prayer, believing, ye shall receive."

You will also be able to give an answer to everyone who asks you questions concerning your faith in the Word of God and the blessed hope you have in the present and in the future.

Jesus gave the parable of the two sons. One son promises the father he would do what he had asked, but he did not keep his word. The second son said he was not going to do what his father asked, but later had a repentant spirit and he repented and carried out his father wishes. When God the Father sends the message of the gospel of Jesus Christ to the Jews, who were God's chosen people; they were called to obey their Father and to carry the gospel to the world. Their forefathers were in covenant with God to welcome the Son of God into the world and to spread His gospel.

However; when the Son of God came into the world, the Jews did not do what they said they would do. The Gentiles received Jesus according to John 1:12 which read, "But as many as received him, to them gave he power to become the sons of God, even to them that believe on his name."

In the past, they were an outcast and they did not agree with the Father that they would spread the gospel of Jesus Christ. But once they became sons of God, they repented and they began to spread the gospel of Jesus Christ. Jesus had this to say about them in Matthew 21:31-32…

> *"Whether of them twain did the will of his father? They say unto him, The first. Jesus saith unto them, Verily I say unto you, That the publicans and the harlots go into the kingdom of God before you. For John came unto you in the way of righteousness, and ye believed him not: but the publicans and the harlots believed him: and ye, when ye had seen it, repented not afterward, that ye might believe him."*

Jesus spoke another parable to His disciples of a householder who did all of the prior preparation needed for his winepress to bear fruit. He hired husbandmen to care for his winepress while he was away. He left and went into a far country. While the householder was away, the husbandmen took his servants and beat one, killed another and stoned another.

The householder received the news and he sent other servants and they did the same thing to those servants also. Finally, he sent his son. He thought they would honor and obey his son. How the father's heart must have hurt when he found out they killed his son also. In Matthew 21:38-39, it reads…

> *"But when the husbandmen saw the son, they said among themselves, This is the heir; come, let us kill him, and let us seize on his inheritance. And they caught him, and cast him out of the vineyard, and slew him."*

Jesus now asks a question in verse 40, "When the lord therefore of the vineyard cometh, what will he do unto those husbandmen?" Then, answered Jesus with these words in verse 41, "They say unto him, He will miserably destroy those wicked men, and will let out his vineyard unto other husbandmen, which shall render him the fruits in their seasons."

For over 2000 years, they had rejected the prophets, the priests, the kings and men and women of God whom God had raised up to prepare the children of Israel for the Lord. The day will come when Jesus is going to return and receive the fruit of the harvest. The Jews rejected, stoned and killed God's prophets when they came with a word from God. They had been sent by God to prepare the winepress for the collection of fruit when the householder returns.

God, the Father, loved the world and the Jews so much until He sent His Son, Jesus, into the world to prepare the rose from the dead on the third day. Before He went back to the Father, He gave a promise of sending the Holy Ghost back. He kept His promise. The promise was given by Jesus in Acts 1:8 which reads, "But ye shall receive power, after that the Holy Ghost is come upon you: and ye shall be witnesses unto me both in Jerusalem, and in all Judaea, and in Samaria, and unto the uttermost part of the earth."

The fulfillment of that promise came on the day of Pentecost. It is written in Acts 2:17-18 which reads…

> *"And it shall come to pass in the last days, saith God, I will pour out of my Spirit upon all flesh: and your sons and your daughters shall prophesy, and your young men shall see visions, and your old men shall dream dreams: And on my servants and on my handmaidens I will pour out in those days of my Spirit; and they shall prophesy."*

Through the power of Holy Spirit many sons were brought into the kingdom of God. These sons of God had received power to produce the fruit of righteousness. Now, when Jesus returns; He will be able to receive us unto Himself and present us to God, the Father. My question to you is, "Are you producing the fruit of righteousness?" It is not by your power neither is it by your might, but it is by the Spirit of God you will produce fruit.

Christ is living in you and if you will allow Him, He will reveal Himself through you. God is not looking for perfect vessels, but He is looking for vessels that will yield themselves to Him. If you will yield yourself to Him, He will produce the fruit in its season.

Jesus said in Matthew 21:42-44…

> *"Jesus saith unto them, Did ye never read in the scriptures, The stone which the builders rejected, the same is become the head of the corner: this is the Lord's doing, and it is marvellous in our eyes? Therefore say I unto you, The kingdom of God shall be taken from you, and given to a nation bringing forth the fruits thereof. And whosoever shall fall on this stone shall be broken: but on whomsoever it shall fall, it will grind him to powder."*

MATTHEW CHAPTER TWENTY-ONE
QUESTIONS FOR APPLICATION

1. Did you pray before you read Matthew chapter twenty-one?
_____

2. Complete a brief summary on "The Mount of Olives"
_____
_____
_____
_____

3. How many disciples did Jesus sent into the village?
_____

4. What did Jesus tell the disciples they were going to find in the village? _____
_____

5. Why did Jesus tell the disciples to bring what they had found in the village to Him? _____
_____

6. Define "Hosanna" _____
_____

7. Where in the Old Testament will you find the word "Hosanna"?
_____

8. When Jesus came into Jerusalem, who did the multitude say He was? _____
_____

9. What did Jesus say could move a mountain? _____
_____

10. Read the parable of the two sons and explain the parable. ____

23

_____
_____
_____
_____

11. Read the parable of the householder and the fruit. Write the spiritual insight Holy Spirit has given you.

_____
_____
_____
_____

NOTE: After reading chapter twenty-one, give three truths you have learned that you can apply to your everyday life to help you produce fruit.

1._____

2._____

3._____

MATTHEW CHAPTER TWENTY-TWO

"And Jesus answered and spake unto them again by parables, and said, The kingdom of heaven is like unto a certain king, which made a marriage for his son, And sent forth his servants to call them that were bidden to the wedding: and they would not come. Again, he sent forth other servants, saying, Tell them which are bidden, Behold, I have prepared my dinner: my oxen and my fatlings are killed, and all things are ready: come unto the marriage. But they made light of it, and went their ways, one to his farm, another to his merchandise: And the remnant took his servants, and entreated them spitefully, and slew them. But when the king heard thereof, he was wroth: and he sent forth his armies, and destroyed those murderers, and burned up their city. Then saith he to his servants, The wedding is ready, but they which were bidden were not worthy. Go ye therefore into the highways, and as many as ye shall find, bid to the marriage. So those servants went out into the highways, and gathered together all as many as they found, both bad and good: and the wedding was furnished with guests. And when the king came in to see the guests, he saw there a man which had not on a wedding garment: And he saith unto him, Friend, how camest thou in hither not having a wedding garment? And he was speechless. Then said the king to the servants, Bind him hand and foot, and take him away, and cast him into outer darkness; there shall be weeping and gnashing of teeth. For many are called, but few are chosen. Then went the Pharisees, and took counsel how they might entangle him in his talk. And they sent out unto him their disciples with the Herodians, saying, Master, we know that thou art true, and teachest the way of God in truth, neither carest thou for any man: for thou regardest not the person of men. Tell us therefore, What thinkest thou? Is it lawful to give tribute unto Caesar, or not? But Jesus perceived their wickedness, and said, Why tempt ye me, ye hypocrites? Shew me the tribute money. And they brought unto him a penny. And he saith unto them, Whose is this image and superscription? They say unto him, Caesar's. Then saith he unto them, Render therefore unto Caesar the things which are Caesar's; and unto God the things that are God's. When they had heard these words, they marvelled, and left him, and went their way. The same day came to him the Sadducees, which say that there is no resurrection, and asked him, Saying, Master, Moses said, If a man die, having no children, his brother shall marry his wife,

and raise up seed unto his brother. Now there were with us seven brethren: and the first, when he had married a wife, deceased, and, having no issue, left his wife unto his brother: Likewise the second also, and the third, unto the seventh. And last of all the woman died also. Therefore in the resurrection whose wife shall she be of the seven? for they all had her. Jesus answered and said unto them, Ye do err, not knowing the scriptures, nor the power of God. For in the resurrection they neither marry, nor are given in marriage, but are as the angels of God in heaven. But as touching the resurrection of the dead, have ye not read that which was spoken unto you by God, saying, I am the God of Abraham, and the God of Isaac, and the God of Jacob? God is not the God of the dead, but of the living. And when the multitude heard this, they were astonished at his doctrine. But when the Pharisees had heard that he had put the Sadducees to silence, they were gathered together. Then one of them, which was a lawyer, asked him a question, tempting him, and saying, Master, which is the great commandment in the law? Jesus said unto him, Thou shalt love the Lord thy God with all thy heart, and with all thy soul, and with all thy mind. This is the first and great commandment. And the second is like unto it, Thou shalt love thy neighbour as thyself. On these two commandments hang all the law and the prophets. While the Pharisees were gathered together, Jesus asked them, Saying, What think ye of Christ? whose son is he? They say unto him, The Son of David. He saith unto them, How then doth David in spirit call him Lord, saying, The LORD said unto my Lord, Sit thou on my right hand, till I make thine enemies thy footstool? If David then call him Lord, how is he his son? And no man was able to answer him a word, neither durst any man from that day forth ask him any more questions."

MATTHEW CHAPTER TWENTY-TWO
"LOVE THE LORD THY GOD"

WORD OF FAITH SCRIPTURES FOR MEDITATION:
Matthew 22:37-40

> *"Jesus said unto him, Thou shalt love the Lord thy God with all thy heart, and with all thy soul, and with all thy mind. This is the first and great commandment. And the second is like unto it, Thou shalt love thy neighbour as thyself. On these two commandments hang all the law and the prophets."*

WORD OF GOD MESSAGE FOR APPLICATION:

After you have read chapter twenty-two prayerfully, God only asks one thing of us. That is to love Him and be clothed with righteousness. He demonstrated His love to us while we were yet sinners. God demonstrated His love for the world by giving His only Son to die on the cross for the sins of the world. It is written in John 3:16-17…

> *"For God so loved the world, that he gave his only begotten Son, that whosoever believeth in him should not perish, but have everlasting life. For God sent not his Son into the world to condemn the world; but that the world through him might be saved."*

When Jesus gave the parable of the king preparing a marriage for his sons and the nations rejected him, He was speaking of those throughout the age who rejected God's Son, Jesus. In John 1:11-13, we read…

> *"He came unto his own, and his own received him not. But as many as received him, to them gave he power to become the sons of God, even to them that believe on his name: Which were born, not of blood, nor of the will of the flesh, nor of the will of man, but of God."*

His own people were the Jews. In the Old Testament, God sent prophets to the children of Israel to warn them when they disobeyed the law of God, which Moses had received from God. God's love for Israel caused God to continue to show His love and mercy to His chosen people. They rejected God's Word. The Old Testament concluded with Israel rejecting God.

Between the Old Testament and the New Testament, history tells us there are 400 years. These 400 years are called silent years. They were silent years because God did not send a prophet to speak into the lives of Israel. God did not forget His people. God was waiting for the fullness of time to arrive. The Apostle Paul wrote in Galatians 4:4-6, which reads…

> "But when the fulness of the time was come, God sent forth his Son, made of a woman, made under the law, To redeem them that were under the law, that we might receive the adoption of sons. And because ye are sons, God hath sent forth the Spirit of his Son into your hearts, crying, Abba, Father."

God, through His great love for the world, gave His Son and His Son gave His life to bring us into son-ship. Now, that we are sons of God; He has made provisions also for us to be clothed with righteousness. Through the power of Holy Ghost, the blood of Jesus and the Word of God, we can live a righteous life.

God loved the world and He gave His Son. We should love God and keep His commandments. I am not speaking of the Ten Commandments Moses received from God the second time. It is written in 1 John 5:3,

> "For this is the love of God, that we keep his commandments: and his commandments are not grievous."

God's commandments are God's Word. The Word of God has been given to us to help us grow in our faith and love for God. In Romans 10:17, we read, "So then faith cometh by hearing, and hearing by the Word of God." Jesus in His grace, love and mercy is touched by our faith and our dependency upon His Word.

It is not His will that the laws of God's Word are honored more than the Lord. The Lord of the letter is Jesus. He will give you the power to obey the commandments of God. The commandments of God are His Word.

God is not going to force us to serve and obey Him. We should love and obey Him just because He first loved us and Jesus died on the cross where He shed His blood to redeem us.

You do not practice sin, but if you missed the mark to obey God's Word; you must repent. When you repent, you are godly sorrowful for your sins. You admit you have sin and then you forsake that sin because you love God. Because of the blood of Jesus, you have been justified. It is as if you have never sinned.

In 1 John 2: 1-2, John wrote…

> *"My little children, these things write I unto you, that ye sin not. And if any man sin, we have an advocate with the Father, Jesus Christ the righteous: And he is the propitiation for our sins: and not for ours only, but also for the sins of the whole world."*

When Jesus was asked which was the great commandment in the law? Jesus answered him with these words from Matthew 22:37 which read, "…Thou shalt love the Lord thy God with all thy heart, and with all thy soul, and with all thy mind."

God demonstrated His love for us while we were yet sinners. He gave His Son and His Son gave His life. One day Jesus will return on a cloud, every eye shall see Him and we shall forever be with the Lord. Even so Lord Jesus, come.

John 15:13 read, "Greater love hath no man than this, that a man lay down his life for his friends." Jesus laid down His life for you. Those who try to bring you into bondage with more law; you must believe the Lord of the Scriptures.

MATTHEW CHAPTER TWENTY-TWO
QUESTIONS FOR APPLICATION

1. When a certain king made a marriage for his son, what was the reaction of those he had invited to the marriage? _____
_____
_____

2. After those who were invited rejected the father's invitation, what did the father tell his servant to do? _____
_____
_____

3. Where did the servants find guest for the wedding? _____
_____
_____

4. When the father came in to see the guest, what did he find? _____
_____
_____

5. What did the king tell the servants to do with the man? _____
_____
_____

NOTE: Jesus has called everyone to the Marriage Supper of the Lamb. You must be washed in the blood of the Lamb and be clothed in righteousness. To be clothed in righteousness is to have Jesus Christ as your Lord and Savior. "For many are called, but few are chosen." (Matthew 22:14)

6. Who were the Herodians? _____
_____

NOTE: They were the political leaders of Jesus' day. They were loyal to Herod whether he was right or wrong in the laws he set forth. In the midst of corruptions, (it does not matter where you find it), you must never support it. Your guidelines are found in God's Word.

> *"...Render therefore unto Caesar the things which are Caesar's; and unto God the things that are God's."*
> **Matthew 22:21**

MATTHEW CHAPTER TWENTY-THREE

"Then spake Jesus to the multitude, and to his disciples, Saying, The scribes and the Pharisees sit in Moses' seat: All therefore whatsoever they bid you observe, that observe and do; but do not ye after their works: for they say, and do not. For they bind heavy burdens and grievous to be borne, and lay them on men's shoulders; but they themselves will not move them with one of their fingers. But all their works they do for to be seen of men: they make broad their phylacteries, and enlarge the borders of their garments, And love the uppermost rooms at feasts, and the chief seats in the synagogues, And greetings in the markets, and to be called of men, Rabbi, Rabbi. But be not ye called Rabbi: for one is your Master, even Christ; and all ye are brethren. And call no man your father upon the earth: for one is your Father, which is in heaven. Neither be ye called masters: for one is your Master, even Christ. But he that is greatest among you shall be your servant. And whosoever shall exalt himself shall be abased; and he that shall humble himself shall be exalted. But woe unto you, scribes and Pharisees, hypocrites! for ye shut up the kingdom of heaven against men: for ye neither go in yourselves, neither suffer ye them that are entering to go in. Woe unto you, scribes and Pharisees, hypocrites! for ye devour widows' houses, and for a pretence make long prayer: therefore ye shall receive the greater damnation. Woe unto you, scribes and Pharisees, hypocrites! for ye compass sea and land to make one proselyte, and when he is made, ye make him twofold more the child of hell than yourselves. Woe unto you, ye blind guides, which say, Whosoever shall swear by the temple, it is nothing; but whosoever shall swear by the gold of the temple, he is a debtor! Ye fools and blind: for whether is greater, the gold, or the temple that sanctifieth the gold? And, Whosoever shall swear by the altar, it is nothing; but whosoever sweareth by the gift that is upon it, he is guilty. Ye fools and blind: for whether is greater, the gift, or the altar that sanctifieth the gift? Whoso therefore shall swear by the altar, sweareth by it, and by all things thereon. And whoso shall swear by the temple, sweareth by it, and by him that dwelleth therein. And he that shall swear by heaven, sweareth by the throne of God, and by him that sitteth thereon. Woe unto you, scribes and Pharisees, hypocrites! for ye pay tithe of mint and anise and cummin, and have omitted the weightier matters of the law, judgment, mercy, and faith: these ought ye to have done, and *not to leave the other undone. Ye blind guides, which strain at a gnat, and swallow a camel. Woe unto you, scribes and Pharisees, hypocrites! for ye make clean the outside of the cup and of the platter, but within they are full of extortion and excess. Thou blind Pharisee, cleanse first that which is within the cup and platter, that the outside of them may be clean also. Woe unto you, scribes and Pharisees, hypocrites! for ye are like unto whited sepulchres, which indeed appear beautiful outward, but are within full of dead men's bones, and of all uncleanness. Even so ye also outwardly appear righteous unto men, but within ye are full of hypocrisy and iniquity. Woe unto you, scribes and Pharisees, hypocrites! because ye build the tombs of the prophets, and garnish the sepulchres of the righteous, And say, If we had been in the days of our fathers, we would not have been partakers with them in the blood of the prophets. Wherefore ye be witnesses unto yourselves, that ye are the children of them which killed the prophets. Fill ye up then the measure of your fathers. Ye serpents, ye generation of vipers, how can ye escape the damnation of hell? Wherefore, behold, I send unto you prophets, and wise men, and scribes: and some of them ye shall kill and crucify; and some of them shall ye scourge in your synagogues, and persecute them from city to city: That upon you may come all the righteous blood shed upon the earth, from the blood of righteous Abel unto the blood of Zacharias son of Barachias, whom ye slew between the temple and the altar. Verily I say unto you, All these things shall come upon this generation. O Jerusalem, Jerusalem, thou that killest the prophets, and stonest them which are sent unto thee, how often would I have gathered thy children together, even as a hen gathereth her chickens under her wings, and ye would not! Behold, your house is left unto you desolate. For I say unto you, Ye shall not see me henceforth, till ye shall say, Blessed is he that cometh in the name of the Lord."*

MATTHEW CHAPTER TWENTY-THREE
"BLESSED IS HE THAT COMETH IN THE NAME OF THE LORD"

WORD OF FAITH SCRIPTURES FOR MEDITATION:
Matthew 23:39

"For I say unto you, Ye shall not see me henceforth, till ye shall say, Blessed is he that cometh in the name of the Lord."

WORD OF GOD MESSAGE FOR APPLICATION:

Jesus knew how it felt to be rejected. Here in chapter twenty-three, Jesus begins teaching His disciples how to recognize and deal with rejection. Rejection begins with isolation and unrealistic expectations. The Scribes and the Pharisees set themselves up as followers of the laws Moses had received from God. Jesus taught His disciples how to recognize the bondage religious leaders will try to bring you under as a Christian. These unrealistic expectations were not the will of God. They were given to Moses by God to teach God's people the love of God and how to live as God's kingdom people.

Jesus said in Matthew 23:3, "All therefore whatsoever they bid you observe, that observe and do; but do not ye after their works: for they say, and do not." In verses 4-36, Jesus teaches of the danger of the law when it is misinterpret. When the law is taught to glorify man, it will bring you into bondage, guilt and fear.
They tried to accuse Jesus of trying to destroy the law. Jesus said in Matthew 5:17, "…He did not come to destroy the law…but to fulfill." Through the power of Holy Spirit and our love for God, we obey Him simply because we love Him.

Through the teaching of the law, which is the Word of God, your mind is being renewed every time you study God's Word. With a renewed mind, you will begin to grow in your faith in God and you will choose to obey Him out of love. Never allow anyone to bring you under the bondage of the law of man. You must remember Jesus shed His blood on Calvary for the sins of the world. We have been set free. "If the Son therefore shall make you free, ye shall be free indeed." (John 8:36)

We have been set free from the influence and power of sin through our Lord Jesus Christ. You must believe Romans 8:1, "There is therefore now no condemnation to them which are in Christ Jesus, who walk not after the flesh, but after the Spirit." The Spirit is the Word of God. Jesus said in John 6:63b, "…the words that I speak unto you, they are spirit, and they are life."

The law was not giving to bring you into bondage, but the law through the power of Holy Spirit and the blood of Jesus, teaches you to live a Christ-empowered life. In Romans 6:1, a question was asked and I will ask you that same question and give you the answer. The Apostle Paul wrote, "What shall we say then? Shall we continue in sin, that grace may abound?" The answer is, "God forbid." (Romans 6:2a)

Jesus continues to demonstrate how to love without limits by interceding in prayer over Jerusalem. They had rejected Him and now He prays for Jerusalem with these words in Matthew 23:37-39 which reads…

> *"O Jerusalem, Jerusalem, thou that killest the prophets, and stonest them which are sent unto thee, how often would I have gathered thy children together, even as a hen gathereth her chickens under her wings, and ye would not! Behold, your house is left unto you desolate. For I say unto you, Ye shall not see me henceforth, till ye shall say, Blessed is he that cometh in the name of the Lord."*

Can you love beyond limits? Will you forgive leaders who have tried to bring you into bondage by giving you unrealistic expectations as a Christian? When you can love beyond limits, God will bless you to reach out and be a blessing to others through your Christian life.

MATTHEW CHAPTER TWENTY-THREE
QUESTIONS FOR APPLICATION

1. Do you obey the Word of God you know when a minister teaches the Word but do not obey the Word? _____
_____

2. What are your reactions when you observe a leader or minister do what they are doing to be seen of men? _____
_____
_____

3. Who did Jesus say was your teacher? _____
_____

NOTE: All teachers who teach the Word of God through the love of God, these are to become your teachers.

4. What will Jesus do for you when you humble ourself? _____
_____
_____

5. Define the word "woe" _____
_____

6. How many "woes" did Jesus speak over the Scribes and Pharisees?
_____

7. It is not the will of God that any be lost. Jesus our great intercessor is praying for us just as He prayed for the city of _____
_____.

8. What was Jesus' response to heavy burdens? _____
_____
_____
_____

9. What things Jesus say will come upon this generation? _____
_____
_____
_____

10. What area of your life has Jesus taken control over through this lesson? _____
_____
_____
_____

MATTHEW CHAPTER TWENTY-FOUR

"And Jesus went out, and departed from the temple: and his disciples came to him for to shew him the buildings of the temple. And Jesus said unto them, See ye not all these things? verily I say unto you, There shall not be left here one stone upon another, that shall not be thrown down. And as he sat upon the mount of Olives, the disciples came unto him privately, saying, Tell us, when shall these things be? and what shall be the sign of thy coming, and of the end of the world? And Jesus answered and said unto them, Take heed that no man deceive you. For many shall come in my name, saying, I am Christ; and shall deceive many. And ye shall hear of wars and rumours of wars: see that ye be not troubled: for all these things must come to pass, but the end is not yet. For nation shall rise against nation, and kingdom against kingdom: and there shall be famines, and pestilences, and earthquakes, in divers places. All these are the beginning of sorrows. Then shall they deliver you up to be afflicted, and shall kill you: and ye shall be hated of all nations for my name's sake. And then shall many be offended, and shall betray one another, and shall hate one another. And many false prophets shall rise, and shall deceive many. And because iniquity shall abound, the love of many shall wax cold. But he that shall endure unto the end, the same shall be saved. And this gospel of the kingdom shall be preached in all the world for a witness unto all nations; and then shall the end come. When ye therefore shall see the abomination of desolation, spoken of by Daniel the prophet, stand in the holy place, (whoso readeth, let him understand:) Then let them which be in Judaea flee into the mountains: Let him which is on the housetop not come down to take any thing out of his house: Neither let him which is in the field return back to take his clothes. And woe unto them that are with child, and to them that give suck in those days! But pray ye that your flight be not in the winter, neither on the sabbath day: For then shall be great tribulation, such as was not since the beginning of the world to this time, no, nor ever shall be. And except those days should be shortened, there should no flesh be saved: but for the elect's sake those days shall be shortened. Then if any man shall say unto you, Lo, here is Christ, or there; believe it not. For there shall arise false Christs, and false prophets, and shall shew great signs and wonders; insomuch that, if it were possible, they shall deceive the very elect. Behold, I have told you before. Wherefore if they shall say unto you, Behold, he is in the desert; go not forth: behold, he is in the secret chambers; believe it not. For as the lightning cometh out of the east, and shineth even unto the west; so shall also the coming of the Son of man be. For wheresoever the carcase is, there will the eagles be gathered together. Immediately after the tribulation of those days shall the sun be darkened, and the moon shall not give her light, and the stars shall fall from heaven, and the powers of the heavens shall be shaken: And then shall appear the sign of the Son of man in heaven: and then shall all the tribes of the earth mourn, and they shall see the Son of man coming in the clouds of heaven with power and great glory. And he shall send his angels with a great sound of a trumpet, and they shall gather together his elect from the four winds, from one end of heaven to the other. Now learn a parable of the fig tree; When his branch is yet tender, and putteth forth leaves, ye know that summer is nigh: So likewise ye, when ye shall see all these things, know that it is near, even at the doors. Verily I say unto you, This generation shall not pass, till all these things be fulfilled. Heaven and earth shall pass away, but my words shall not pass away. But of that day and hour knoweth no man, no, not the angels of heaven, but my Father only. But as the days of Noe were, so shall also the coming of the Son of man be. For as in the days that were before the flood they were eating and drinking, marrying and giving in marriage, until the day that Noe entered into the ark, And knew not until the flood came, and took them all away; so shall also the coming of the Son of man be. Then shall two be in the field; the one shall be taken, and the other left. Two women shall be grinding at the mill; the one shall be taken, and the other left. Watch therefore: for ye know not what hour your Lord doth come. But know this, that if the goodman of the house had known in what watch the thief would come, he would have watched, and would not have suffered his house to be broken up. Therefore be ye also ready: for in such an hour as ye think not the Son of man cometh. Who then is a faithful and wise servant, whom his lord hath made ruler over his household, to give them meat in due season? Blessed is that servant, whom his lord when he cometh shall find so doing. Verily I say unto you, That he shall make him ruler over all his goods. But and if that evil servant shall say in his heart, My lord delayeth his coming; And shall begin to smite his fellowservants, and to eat and drink with the drunken; The lord of that servant shall come in a day when he looketh not for him, and in an hour that he is not aware of, And shall cut him asunder, and *appoint him his portion with the hypocrites: there shall be weeping and gnashing of teeth."*

MATTHEW CHAPTER TWENTY-FOUR
"WHAT SHALL BE THE SIGN OF HIS COMING?"

WORD OF FAITH SCRIPTURES FOR MEDITATION:
Matthew 24:3-4

"And as he sat upon the mount of Olives, the disciples came unto him privately, saying, Tell us, when shall these things be? and what shall be the sign of thy coming, and of the end of the world? And Jesus answered and said unto them, Take heed that no man deceive you."

WORD OF GOD MESSAGE FOR APPLICATION:

It is not, if Jesus will return; it is when Jesus will return. He will return in glory and Jesus will demonstrate His power over all power of the devil. Until that day comes, Jesus said in Luke 19:13, "…Occupy till I come." In Matthew 24:36, we read, "But of that day and hour knoweth no man, no, not the angels of heaven, but my Father only."

No one but God knows the day and hour Jesus will return. We have heard many false prophets who wrote books and set a date Jesus would return. Those dates they predicted have come and gone and Jesus has not returned. Do not think He will not return. He shall return as a thief in the night.
Jesus said in Matthew 24:4, "…Take heed that no man deceive you." That word "deceive" means "to seduce wholly; to lead astray." To keep you from being seduced or led astray, Jesus teaches on the signs of the time. I will not include an in-depth study on the signs of the time, but I will list many of the signs Jesus listed.

Jesus does not want you to become misinformed. When you read the list of the signs of the time, listen to the news and read the newspaper to see how many of the signs of time you can find.

SIGNS OF THE TIME:

1. "For many shall come in my name, saying, I am Christ…" (Matthew 24:5a)

2. "And ye shall hear of wars and rumours of wars…" (Matthew 24:6a)

Jesus said, "…see that ye be not troubled: for all these things must come to pass, but the end is not yet." (Matthew 24:6b)

3. "For nation shall rise against nation, and kingdom against kingdom…" (Matthew 24:7a)

4. "… there shall be famines…" (Matthew 24:7b)

5. "…pestilences…" (Matthew 24:7b)

6. "…earthquakes in divers places." (Matthew 24:7b)

"All these are the beginning of sorrows." (Matthew 24:8) As you read chapter 24, write the signs of the time you will find during your study of the Scriptures.

Jesus gave every born-again Christian their divine assignment. He said in Matthew 24:14, "And this gospel of the kingdom shall be preached in all the world for a witness unto all nations; and then shall the end come."

Your divine assignment is to preach. That word "preach" in the Greek is "euaggelizo" which means "to announce good news" (the gospel). Announce the good news according to John 3:16-17…

> "For God so loved the world, that he gave his only begotten Son, that whosoever believeth in him should not perish, but have everlasting life. For God sent not his Son into the world to condemn the world; but that the world through him might be saved."

After Jesus comes on the cloud according to Acts 1:9-11 which reads…

> "And when he had spoken these things, while they beheld, he was taken up; and a cloud received him out of their sight. And while they looked stedfastly toward heaven as he went up, behold, two men stood by them in white apparel; Which also said, Ye men of Galilee, why stand ye gazing up into heaven? this same Jesus, which is taken up from you into heaven, shall so come in like manner as ye have seen him go into heaven."

There will be tribulation upon the earth. This is according to Matthew 24:15-28. Jesus continues to teach of His coming in Matthew 24:29-31. In verses 32-36, Jesus taught about the fig tree. In the midst of His teachings, He interjected the everlasting power of God's Word. "Heaven and earth shall pass away, but my words shall not pass away." (Matthew 24:35)

There is power in the Word of God. Before Joshua entered the promise land, God told Joshua the power of his success would depend on these verses written in Joshua 1:8-9 which read…

> "This book of the law shall not depart out of thy mouth; but thou shalt meditate therein day and night, that thou mayest observe to do according to all that is written therein: for then thou shalt make thy way prosperous, and then thou shalt have good success. Have not I commanded thee? Be strong and of a good courage; be not afraid, neither be thou dismayed: for the LORD thy God is with thee whithersoever thou goest."

The Word of God has power to fill you and that Word has power to heal you. If you are going to have good success, you must meditate on God's Word day and night. As you meditate upon God's Word, you are renewing your mind and you are also adding to your faith. As your faith begins to grow, you will speak God's Word into every situation that does not agree with the Word of God.

God gave us a command to occupy until He returns. To occupy is to do the Lord's business until He comes. As you occupy until the Lord returns, do not allow the devil to deceive you. Just because there has been a delay in Jesus' return; He shall return. In Matthew 24:42, we read, "Watch therefore: for ye know not what hour your Lord doth come."

"Watch" means "to be mentally and physically alert." As the final hour approaches, "Watch therefore: for ye know not what hour your Lord doth come." It is not the will of God for you to watch in fear if you are a child of God. Jesus said in John 16:33, "These things I have spoken unto you, that in me ye might have peace. In the world ye shall have tribulation: but be of good cheer; I have overcome the world."

Those in the world shall have tribulation. Let me interject this from the Lord. It is not the will of God that any be lost or goes through the tribulation that shall come upon the world. Take a few minutes out of your busy schedule to bring them to Christ. No one wants to go through the tribulation that shall come upon the earth; and no one, young or old, has a desire to die without Jesus. They do not know it now, but deep down in their heart they also desire to spend eternity in heaven.

When you received Jesus as Savior and Lord of your life, you became God's child and Jesus will return for the children of God. "Therefore be ye also ready: for in such an hour as ye think not the Son of man cometh." (Matthew 24:44)

MATTHEW CHAPTER TWENTY-FOUR
QUESTIONS FOR APPLICATION

I. Before you leave home each day, you must take a few minutes to prepare yourself. Before Jesus returns on a cloud, you must also prepare yourself for His return. Give four things everyone must do to be prepared for Jesus' return. Give Scripture. The Scripture can be taken from any place in God's Word.

1._____

2._____

3._____

4._____

5. Does anyone know the day or the hour when Jesus will return? __
_____

II. Give three signs of the time that has already come to pass.

6. _____

7. _____

8. _____

9. Are you ready for Jesus to return? _____
10. If you have received Jesus as Savior and Lord of your life, then you are ready for Jesus' return.

Never allow the devil to cause you to live your life in fear and condemnation. God loves you and His perfect will for your life until Jesus returns is to live a life of victory, peace, joy and power through the Holy Ghost. It is written in Romans 8:1, "There is therefore now no condemnation to them which are in Christ Jesus, who walk not after the flesh, but after the Spirit."

When you sin, you have missed the mark. Everyone will miss the mark, but you do not practice sin. You are a New Creature in Christ. Never forget, God loves you. In 1 John 5:3-5, we read…

> *"For this is the love of God, that we keep his commandments: and his commandments are not grievous. For whatsoever is born of God overcometh the world: and this is the victory that overcometh the world, even our faith. Who is he that overcometh the world, but he that believeth that Jesus is the Son of God?"*

Now, live a victorious, blessed and prosperous life as you wait for the return of Jesus.

MATTHEW CHAPTER TWENTY-FIVE

"Then shall the kingdom of heaven be likened unto ten virgins, which took their lamps, and went forth to meet the bridegroom. And five of them were wise, and five were foolish. They that were foolish took their lamps, and took no oil with them: But the wise took oil in their vessels with their lamps. While the bridegroom tarried, they all slumbered and slept. And at midnight there was a cry made, Behold, the bridegroom cometh; go ye out to meet him. Then all those virgins arose, and trimmed their lamps. And the foolish said unto the wise, Give us of your oil; for our lamps are gone out. But the wise answered, saying, Not so; lest there be not enough for us and you: but go ye rather to them that sell, and buy for yourselves. And while they went to buy, the bridegroom came; and they that were ready went in with him to the marriage: and the door was shut. Afterward came also the other virgins, saying, Lord, Lord, open to us. But he answered and said, Verily I say unto you, I know you not. Watch therefore, for ye know neither the day nor the hour wherein the Son of man cometh. For the kingdom of heaven is as a man travelling into a far country, who called his own servants, and delivered unto them his goods. And unto one he gave five talents, to another two, and to another one; to every man according to his several ability; and straightway took his journey. Then he that had received the five talents went and traded with the same, and made them other five talents. And likewise he that had received two, he also gained other two. But he that had received one went and digged in the earth, and hid his lord's money. After a long time the lord of those servants cometh, and reckoneth with them. And so he that had received five talents came and brought other five talents, saying, Lord, thou deliveredst unto me five talents: behold, I have gained beside them five talents more. His lord said unto him, Well done, thou good and faithful servant: thou hast been faithful over a few things, I will make thee ruler over many things: enter thou into the joy of thy lord. He also that had received two talents came and said, Lord, thou deliveredst unto me two talents: behold, I have gained two other talents beside them. His lord said unto him, Well done, good and faithful servant; thou hast been faithful over a few things, I will make thee ruler over many things: enter thou into the joy of thy lord. Then he which had received the one talent came and said, Lord, I knew thee that thou art an hard man, reaping where thou hast not sown, and gathering where thou hast

not strawed: And I was afraid, and went and hid thy talent in the earth: lo, there thou hast that is thine. His lord answered and said unto him, Thou wicked and slothful servant, thou knewest that I reap where I sowed not, and gather where I have not strawed: Thou oughtest therefore to have put my money to the exchangers, and then at my coming I should have received mine own with usury. Take therefore the talent from him, and give it unto him which hath ten talents. For unto every one that hath shall be given, and he shall have abundance: but from him that hath not shall be taken away even that which he hath. And cast ye the unprofitable servant into outer darkness: there shall be weeping and gnashing of teeth. When the Son of man shall come in his glory, and all the holy angels with him, then shall he sit upon the throne of his glory: And before him shall be gathered all nations: and he shall separate them one from another, as a shepherd divideth his sheep from the goats: And he shall set the sheep on his right hand, but the goats on the left. Then shall the King say unto them on his right hand, Come, ye blessed of my Father, inherit the kingdom prepared for you from the foundation of the world: For I was an hungred, and ye gave me meat: I was thirsty, and ye gave me drink: I was a stranger, and ye took me in: Naked, and ye clothed me: I was sick, and ye visited me: I was in prison, and ye came unto me. Then shall the righteous answer him, saying, Lord, when saw we thee an hungred, and fed thee? or thirsty, and gave thee drink? When saw we thee a stranger, and took thee in? or naked, and clothed thee? Or when saw we thee sick, or in prison, and came unto thee? And the King shall answer and say unto them, Verily I say unto you, Inasmuch as ye have done it unto one of the least of these my brethren, ye have done it unto me. Then shall he say also unto them on the left hand, Depart from me, ye cursed, into everlasting fire, prepared for the devil and his angels: For I was an hungred, and ye gave me no meat: I was thirsty, and ye gave me no drink: I was a stranger, and ye took me not in: naked, and ye clothed me not: sick, and in prison, and ye visited me not. Then shall they also answer him, saying, Lord, when saw we thee an hungred, or athirst, or a stranger, or naked, or sick, or in prison, and did not minister unto thee? Then shall he answer them, saying, Verily I say unto you, Inasmuch as ye did it not to one of the least of these, ye did it not to me. And these shall go away into everlasting punishment: but the righteous into life eternal."

MATTHEW CHAPTER TWENTY-FIVE
"COME, YE BLESSED OF MY FATHER"

WORD OF FAITH SCRIPTURES FOR MEDITATION:
Matthew 25:31-34

> *"When the Son of man shall come in his glory, and all the holy angels with him, then shall he sit upon the throne of his glory: And before him shall be gathered all nations: and he shall separate them one from another, as a shepherd divideth his sheep from the goats: And he shall set the sheep on his right hand, but the goats on the left. Then shall the King say unto them on his right hand, Come, ye blessed of my Father, inherit the kingdom prepared for you from the foundation of the world."*

WORD OF GOD MESSAGE FOR APPLICATION:

As I travel throughout the United States preaching and teaching the gospel of Jesus Christ, I have found so many born-again Christians suffering. They are faithful, dedicated, committed men and women of God who has been living a faithful Christian life, but they are going through intense suffering.

The questions many ask are why the heartache and pain? Why is it that when I fast and pray in faith, I do not see God answering my prayers?

Let me say to you, there are some questions we will never know the answer to until we see Jesus. One thing I do know is that God will always give you sufficient grace to go through what you are facing. It is not God's perfect will for you or anyone else to suffer. God's perfect will for humanity is found in Genesis 1:26-28 which read…

> *"And God said, Let us make man in our image, after our likeness: and let them have dominion over the fish of the sea, and over the fowl of the air, and over the cattle, and over all the earth, and over every creeping thing that creepeth upon the earth. So God created man in his own image, in the image of God created he him; male*

and female created he them. And God blessed them, and God said unto them, Be fruitful, and multiply, and replenish the earth, and subdue it: and have dominion over the fish of the sea, and over the fowl of the air, and over every living thing that moveth upon the earth."

We are not to blame God for the distress, sickness, tribulation and death we see in the world today. God gave the title deed of the earth to Adam and Eve. He also gave them power and authority to rule the earth. Divine power and authority over the devil is enforced as long as you remain divinely connected to God and daily have fellowship with Him in His presence. In other words, you must pray each day. The cool of the day (I believe) is in the morning. David said in Psalms 63:1, "O God, thou art my God; early will I seek thee: my soul thirsteth for thee, my flesh longeth for thee in a dry and thirsty land, where no water is."

Adam and Eve became disconnected from God when they disobeyed His direct command and obeyed the devil. Adam and Eve had always been connected to God from the day they were created in the image and likeness of God. Sin will separate you from God. Sin is death. God told them the day they disobeyed Him and eat of the tree, they would die. To be separated from God is death. Before Adam and Eve sinned, there was no time. Death operates in the period of life called time.

Before they sinned, they only knew eternity. There is no beginning and end to eternity. God is Eternity. Adam and Eve sinned. After they sinned, they hid themselves from the presence of God. They also transferred ownership of the world over to the devil. He is called the god of this world. In 2 Corinthians 4:3-4, the Apostle Paul wrote...

> *"But if our gospel be hid, it is hid to them that are lost: In whom the god of this world hath blinded the minds of them which believe not, lest the light of the glorious gospel of Christ, who is the image of God, should shine unto them."*

When Adam and Eve disobeyed God's Word, they were giving the devil their title deed to the earth. After Satan received the title deed to the earth, he was able to release a spirit of fear. Adam and Eve never knew fear before; now, they were afraid and they hid themselves from God. They never knew shame; now, they were ashamed and they made leaves to cover themselves.

Adam and Eve were driven out of the presence of God. They had two sons, Cain and Abel. Satan released the seed of jealousy, anger and murder in Cain. He killed his brother, Abel. The seed of Satan was released in the world and death, anger, violence, sickness, fear and etc. began to spread. Satan's plan was to have the world believe it was God's fault. If he could let them believe it was God who created all things, then mankind would become angry with God and serve him.

He must have forgotten the promise God gave to Adam and all of humanity before Adam and Eve was driven out of the garden. I will remind you of God's promise in Genesis 3:15, "And I will put enmity between thee and the woman, and between thy seed and her seed; it shall bruise thy head, and thou shalt bruise his heel."

The seed of the woman is our Lord and Savior Jesus Christ. This is the first promise of a Redeemer stepping out of eternity into time to redeem mankind. This would take place in the fullness of time. In Galatians 4:3-5, the Apostle Paul wrote…

> *"Even so we, when we were children, were in bondage under the elements of the world: But when the fulness of the time was come, God sent forth his Son, made of a woman, made under the law, To redeem them that were under the law, that we might receive the adoption of sons."*

In the fullness of time, Jesus stepped out of time into eternity to bring us back to God. Until Jesus returns the devil will continue to work his evil works throughout the world and also in the air. Jesus said in John 10:10, "The thief cometh not, but for to steal, and to kill, and to destroy: I am come that they might have life, and that they might have it more abundantly."

The only thing that is affected by time and the attacks of the devil is our flesh. The Apostle Paul said in Romans 7:18, "For I know that in me (that is, in my flesh,) dwelleth no good thing…" He also called our flesh "a body of death." (Romans 7:24)

The flesh is a body of death due to sin, but in every born-again Christian lives eternal life. We have Christ in us "…which is Christ in you, the hope of glory." (Colossians 1:27b) The last enemy that will be destroyed is death. Death operates in the spirit of time.

I must show you this mystery in God's Word. My prayer for you is that God will open your eyes to see and your ears to hear the truth of God's eternal plan. There shall be glory after this. There shall be a new body after this. There will be no more devil after this. There will be a new heaven and a new earth after this. In 1 Corinthians 15:51-58, we read…

> *"Behold, I shew you a mystery; We shall not all sleep, but we shall all be changed, In a moment, in the twinkling of an eye, at the last trump: for the trumpet shall sound, and the dead shall be raised incorruptible, and we shall be changed. For this corruptible must put on incorruption, and this mortal must put on immortality. So when this corruptible shall have put on incorruption, and this mortal shall have put on immortality, then shall be brought to pass the saying that is written, Death is swallowed up in victory. O death, where is thy sting? O grave, where is thy victory? The sting of death is sin; and the strength of sin is the law. But thanks be to God, which giveth us the victory through our Lord Jesus Christ. Therefore, my beloved brethren, be ye stedfast, unmoveable, always abounding in the work of the Lord, forasmuch as ye know that your labour is not in vain in the Lord."*

There shall be glory, honor, praise and eternal peace after this. Amen!

MATTHEW CHAPTER TWENTY-FIVE
QUESTIONS FOR APPLICATION

1. What is a parable? _____
_____

2. How many virgins were there? _____

NOTE: One set took oil in their lamps and the other set had lamps but no oil. To meet the bridegroom and be taken to the marriage, you had to have oil. The oil in your life is the Holy Ghost. He will give you the power you will need to live a Spirit-filled life until Jesus returns. Jesus said in Matthew 5:14a, "Ye are the light of the world…"

3. What is the kingdom of heaven compared to?_____
_____

4. Give at least three biblical truths that will take place when the Son of man (Jesus) returns. _____
_____
_____

7. What will the King say to those on His right? _____
_____
_____

8. What were the six things the righteous had done for Jesus that caused Him to say, "Come, ye blessed of my Father, inherit the kingdom prepared for you from the foundation of the world."

_____
_____
_____
_____

MATTHEW CHAPTER TWENTY-SIX

"And it came to pass, when Jesus had finished all these sayings, he said unto his disciples, Ye know that after two days is the feast of the passover, and the Son of man is betrayed to be crucified. Then assembled together the chief priests, and the scribes, and the elders of the people, unto the palace of the high priest, who was called Caiaphas, And consulted that they might take Jesus by subtilty, and kill him. But they said, Not on the feast day, lest there be an uproar among the people. Now when Jesus was in Bethany, in the house of Simon the leper, There came unto him a woman having an alabaster box of very precious ointment, and poured it on his head, as he sat at meat. But when his disciples saw it, they had indignation, saying, To what purpose is this waste? For this ointment might have been sold for much, and given to the poor.
[10] When Jesus understood it, he said unto them, Why trouble ye the woman? for she hath wrought a good work upon me. For ye have the poor always with you; but me ye have not always. For in that she hath poured this ointment on my body, she did it for my burial. Verily I say unto you, Wheresoever this gospel shall be preached in the whole world, there shall also this, that this woman hath done, be told for a memorial of her. Then one of the twelve, called Judas Iscariot, went unto the chief priests, And said unto them, What will ye give me, and I will deliver him unto you? And they covenanted with him for thirty pieces of silver. And from that time he sought opportunity to betray him. Now the first day of the feast of unleavened bread the disciples came to Jesus, saying unto him, Where wilt thou that we prepare for thee to eat the passover? And he said, Go into the city to such a man, and say unto him, The Master saith, My time is at hand; I will keep the passover at thy house with my disciples. And the disciples did as Jesus had appointed them; and they made ready the passover. Now when the even was come, he sat down with the twelve. And as they did eat, he said, Verily I say unto you, that one of you shall betray me. And they were exceeding sorrowful, and began every one of them to say unto him, Lord, is it I? And he answered and said, He that dippeth his hand with me in the dish, the same shall betray me. The Son of man goeth as it is written of him: but woe unto that man by whom the Son of man is betrayed! it had been good for that man if he had not been born. Then Judas, which betrayed him, answered and said, Master, is it I? He said unto him, Thou hast

said. And as they were eating, Jesus took bread, and blessed it, and brake it, and gave it to the disciples, and said, Take, eat; this is my body. And he took the cup, and gave thanks, and gave it to them, saying, Drink ye all of it; For this is my blood of the new testament, which is shed for many for the remission of sins. But I say unto you, I will not drink henceforth of this fruit of the vine, until that day when I drink it new with you in my Father's kingdom. And when they had sung an hymn, they went out into the mount of Olives. Then saith Jesus unto them, All ye shall be offended because of me this night: for it is written, I will smite the shepherd, and the sheep of the flock shall be scattered abroad. But after I am risen again, I will go before you into Galilee. Peter answered and said unto him, Though all men shall be offended because of thee, yet will I never be offended. Jesus said unto him, Verily I say unto thee, That this night, before the cock crow, thou shalt deny me thrice. Peter said unto him, Though I should die with thee, yet will I not deny thee. Likewise also said all the disciples. Then cometh Jesus with them unto a place called Gethsemane, and saith unto the disciples, Sit ye here, while I go and pray yonder. And he took with him Peter and the two sons of Zebedee, and began to be sorrowful and very heavy. Then saith he unto them, My soul is exceeding sorrowful, even unto death: tarry ye here, and watch with me. And he went a little further, and fell on his face, and prayed, saying, O my Father, if it be possible, let this cup pass from me: nevertheless not as I will, but as thou wilt. And he cometh unto the disciples, and findeth them asleep, and saith unto Peter, What, could ye not watch with me one hour? Watch and pray, that ye enter not into temptation: the spirit indeed is willing, but the flesh is weak. He went away again the second time, and prayed, saying, O my Father, if this cup may not pass away from me, except I drink it, thy will be done. And he came and found them asleep again: for their eyes were heavy. And he left them, and went away again, and prayed the third time, saying the same words. Then cometh he to his disciples, and saith unto them, Sleep on now, and take your rest: behold, the hour is at hand, and the Son of man is betrayed into the hands of sinners. Rise, let us be going: behold, he is at hand that doth betray me. And while he yet spake, lo, Judas, one of the twelve, came, and with him a great multitude with swords and staves, from the chief priests and elders of the people. Now he that betrayed him gave them a sign, saying, Whomsoever I shall kiss, that same is he: hold him fast. And forthwith he came to Jesus, and said, Hail, master; and kissed him. And Jesus said unto him, Friend, wherefore art thou come? Then came they, and laid hands on Jesus, and took him. And, behold, one of them which were with Jesus stretched out his hand, and drew his sword, and struck a servant of the high priest's, and smote off his ear. Then said Jesus unto him, Put up again thy sword into his place: for all they that take the sword shall perish with the sword. Thinkest thou that I cannot now pray to my Father, and he shall presently give me more than twelve legions of angels? But how then shall the scriptures be fulfilled, that thus it must be? In that same hour said Jesus to the multitudes, Are ye come out as against a thief with swords and staves for to take me? I sat daily with you teaching in the temple, and ye laid no hold on me. But all this was done, that the scriptures of the prophets might be fulfilled. Then all the disciples forsook him, and fled. And they that had laid hold on Jesus led him away to Caiaphas the high priest, where the scribes and the elders were assembled. But Peter followed him afar off unto the high priest's palace, and went in, and sat with the servants, to see the end. Now the chief priests, and elders, and all the council, sought false witness against Jesus, to put him to death; But found none: yea, though many false witnesses came, yet found they none. At the last came two false witnesses, And said, This fellow said, I am able to destroy the temple of God, and to build it in three days. And the high priest arose, and said unto him, Answerest thou nothing? what is it which these witness against thee? But Jesus held his peace. And the high priest answered and said unto him, I adjure thee by the living God, that thou tell us whether thou be the Christ, the Son of God. Jesus saith unto him, Thou hast said: nevertheless I say unto you, Hereafter shall ye see the Son of man sitting on the right hand of power, and coming in the clouds of heaven. Then the high priest rent his clothes, saying, He hath spoken blasphemy; what further need have we of witnesses? behold, now ye have heard his blasphemy. What think ye? They answered and said, He is guilty of death. Then did they spit in his face, and buffeted him; and others smote him with the palms of their hands, Saying, Prophesy unto us, thou Christ, Who is he that smote thee? Now Peter sat without in the palace: and a damsel came unto him, saying, Thou also wast with Jesus of Galilee. But he denied before them all, saying, I know not what thou sayest. And when he was gone out into the porch, another maid saw him, and said unto them that were there, This fellow was also with Jesus of Nazareth. And again he denied with an oath, I do not know the *man. And after a while came unto him they that stood by, and said to Peter, Surely thou also art one of them; for thy speech bewrayeth thee. Then began he to curse and to swear, saying, I know not the man. And immediately the cock crew. And Peter remembered the word of Jesus, which said unto him, Before the cock crow, thou shalt deny me thrice. And he went out, and wept bitterly."*

MATTHEW CHAPTER TWENTY-SIX
"WATCH AND PRAY THAT YE ENTER NOT INTO TEMPTATION"

WORD OF FAITH SCRIPTURES FOR MEDITATION:
Matthew 26:40-42

"And he cometh unto the disciples, and findeth them asleep, and saith unto Peter, What, could ye not watch with me one hour? Watch and pray, that ye enter not into temptation: the spirit indeed is willing, but the flesh is weak. He went away again the second time, and prayed, saying, O my Father, if this cup may not pass away from me, except I drink it, thy will be done."

WORD OF GOD MESSAGE FOR APPLICATION:

In the inspired, prophetic teaching on prayer, I shared with you a portion of the message I taught at our Prophetic Word of God and Prayer Luncheon. I will share with you the message I received in prayer that morning.

God spoke in my heart and said, "Dorothy, every prayer is important to me and I hear every prayer." Later, God spoke again in my heart and said, "Tell My children prayer gives me an entrance into the earth. I command them to call unto Me and I will answer and show them great and mighty things they know not. When they pray and fast, the power of Satan is destroyed."

As Jesus prayed in Matthew 26:2, He came to the place of prayer where every intercessor will come to in prayer. If we use the pattern of the tabernacle in the wilderness, you will be able to understand where Jesus was the first time He prayed in the Garden of Gethsemane.

Jesus came to the place of separating Himself from the people. In the outer court, there are so many distractions. The people are not your problem. You must not allow them to distract you as you move from the outer court in prayer as you continue to have an ear to hear the Spirit. Jesus, the Son of God; Emmanuel, God with us; who has power over all things and know the end from the beginning became what we are so that we might become who He is in this life.

In Hebrews 4:15-16, the Apostle Paul wrote…

> *"For we have not an high priest which cannot be touched with the feeling of our infirmities; but was in all points tempted like as we are, yet without sin. Let us therefore come boldly unto the throne of grace, that we may obtain mercy, and find grace to help in time of need."*

Jesus demonstrated the power of God when you are interceding in the outer court. Jesus did not allow the distractions to cause Him to continue to pray beyond His sorrow. He began His prayer sorrowful and very heavy. He separated Himself for the second time.

I believe God allowed the spirit of slumber and sleep to come upon them so that they would not try to hinder God's will. Jesus prayed and came into the Holy Place. Jesus released them to sleep on while He went a little further. It was there in the Holy Place that Jesus, the Bread of Life, was there in the Holy Place with the showbread on the left and the candles burning on the other side of Him.

Jesus is the Bread of Life and Jesus is the Light of the World. Jesus who is the illumination that shines upon the bread of His presence as you, the priest of God, continues to follow Jesus in prayer.

You must continue to intercede in prayer until you pray beyond the veil. You were following the example of Jesus when you interceded in the outer court for others. In the outer court of prayer, you know there was a place in God you had not arrived yet. As you looked around at the distractions, you must look at the distractions as Jesus looked at Peter, James and John and said, "Tarry ye here, and watch with me." When those in the outer court does not pray and watch with you, you must go a little further. The cry came from Jesus' sorrowful and very heavy soul.

Jesus prayed from the outer court on into the inner court where the bread of His presence and the light of the Spirit and power of God was. In verses 44-46, Jesus finds His disciples asleep for the third time. This time Jesus entered beyond the third veil of intercession. The first veil you prayed by the seeing of the eye and the hearing of the ear.

As you continue to intercede beyond the second veil, this is where the intercessors pray by the Word of God. As Jesus speaks the word into your heart, you realize as you pray that you are partaking of the bread of His presence. With every revelation of God's Word, you know you have been favored by God with illumination.

By way of the separation and the impartation, now comes the illumination of God's glory as you interceded in prayer beyond the third veil. That veil is a type and shadow of the hand of God. Behind God's hand is His glory. You are not asking God for the things of this natural world. You have come to a place where you have a desire for His glory.

That is the same place Moses was when he called out in intercessory prayer for God to show him His glory. Beyond the third veil is where you enter the glory of God in intercessory prayer. Beyond that veil of the hand of God is where you enter God's glory. You must be persistent in prayer as you intercede. Who knows if God will move His hand so that you can enter the place of His glory.
In Exodus 33:21-23, we read…

> *"And the LORD said, Behold, there is a place by me, and thou shalt stand upon a rock: And it shall come to pass, while my glory passeth by, that I will put thee in a clift of the rock, and will cover thee with my hand while I pass by: And I will take away mine hand, and thou shalt see my back parts: but my face shall not be seen."*

When God moves His hand and you enter into His glory and His presence, you will gladly say as Jesus said in Matthew 26:42b, "…O my Father, if this cup may not pass away from me, except I drink it, thy will be done."

When the veil of God's hand is moved and God allows you to enter into the glory of His presence, it is for you to fulfill the will of God. The process and the pain of glory is when God has removed the veil of His hand.

Jesus was able to go through the betrayal of Judas, one of His disciples. Through the glory of God, Jesus was able to stand before those who had Him on trial. If Jesus had to pray beyond the veil, then we who belong to Jesus must also pray without ceasing.

MATTHEW CHAPTER TWENTY-SIX
QUESTIONS FOR APPLICATION

1. Why was the Son of man betrayed? _____
_____

2. What was the name of the man who Jesus healed from leprosy?
_____

NOTE: Jesus not only heals the man from leprosy, but He went for a visit in the man's home. Leprosy is like sin. When you were in sin, the sin spread through the house of your body. If Jesus had not saved and healed you, progressively you could have been dead; but Jesus healed you and now Jesus lives in your house.

3. When Jesus was visiting the man with leprosy, what did the women do? _____
_____

4. Why did she anoint Jesus? _____
_____

NOTE: Before death takes place, there is suffering and pain. You cannot go through suffering and pain without the anointing. Jesus left us an example. You have Holy Spirit in you, but you need the anointing upon you. The anointing comes upon you as you praise and worship Jesus and also, as you hear God's Word preached and taught.

5. Where did Jesus go to pray in chapter twenty-six?
_____

6. How many times did Jesus pray? _____

NOTE: If Jesus prayed over and over again, you should also pray until you hear from God.

7. What did Jesus tell Peter, James and John to do to keep from entering into temptation? _____
_____

MATTHEW CHAPTER TWENTY-SEVEN

"When the morning was come, all the chief priests and elders of the people took counsel against Jesus to put him to death: And when they had bound him, they led him away, and delivered him to Pontius Pilate the governor. Then Judas, which had betrayed him, when he saw that he was condemned, repented himself, and brought again the thirty pieces of silver to the chief priests and elders, Saying, I have sinned in that I have betrayed the innocent blood. And they said, What is that to us? see thou to that. And he cast down the pieces of silver in the temple, and departed, and went and hanged himself. And the chief priests took the silver pieces, and said, It is not lawful for to put them into the treasury, because it is the price of blood. And they took counsel, and bought with them the potter's field, to bury strangers in. Wherefore that field was called, The field of blood, unto this day. Then was fulfilled that which was spoken by Jeremy the prophet, saying, And they took the thirty pieces of silver, the price of him that was valued, whom they of the children of Israel did value; And gave them for the potter's field, as the Lord appointed me. And Jesus stood before the governor: and the governor asked him, saying, Art thou the King of the Jews? And Jesus said unto him, Thou sayest. And when he was accused of the chief priests and elders, he answered nothing. Then said Pilate unto him, Hearest thou not how many things they witness against thee? And he answered him to never a word; insomuch that the governor marvelled greatly. Now at that feast the governor was wont to release unto the people a prisoner, whom they would. And they had then a notable prisoner, called Barabbas. Therefore when they were gathered together, Pilate said unto them, Whom will ye that I release unto you? Barabbas, or Jesus which is called Christ? For he knew that for envy they had delivered him. When he was set down on the judgment seat, his wife sent unto him, saying, Have thou nothing to do with that just man: for I have suffered many things this day in a dream because of him. But the chief priests and elders persuaded the multitude that they should ask Barabbas, and destroy Jesus. The governor answered and said unto them, Whether of the twain will ye that I release unto you? They said, Barabbas. Pilate saith unto them, What shall I do then with Jesus which is called Christ? They all say unto him, Let him be crucified. And the governor said, Why, what evil hath he done? But they cried out the more, saying, Let him be crucified. When Pilate saw that

he could prevail nothing, but that rather a tumult was made, he took water, and washed his hands before the multitude, saying, I am innocent of the blood of this just person: see ye to it. Then answered all the people, and said, His blood be on us, and on our children. Then released he Barabbas unto them: and when he had scourged Jesus, he delivered him to be crucified. Then the soldiers of the governor took Jesus into the common hall, and gathered unto him the whole band of soldiers. And they stripped him, and put on him a scarlet robe. And when they had platted a crown of thorns, they put it upon his head, and a reed in his right hand: and they bowed the knee before him, and mocked him, saying, Hail, King of the Jews! And they spit upon him, and took the reed, and smote him on the head. And after that they had mocked him, they took the robe off from him, and put his own raiment on him, and led him away to crucify him. And as they came out, they found a man of Cyrene, Simon by name: him they compelled to bear his cross. And when they were come unto a place called Golgotha, that is to say, a place of a skull, They gave him vinegar to drink mingled with gall: and when he had tasted thereof, he would not drink. And they crucified him, and parted his garments, casting lots: that it might be fulfilled which was spoken by the prophet, They parted my garments among them, and upon my vesture did they cast lots. And sitting down they watched him there; And set up over his head his accusation written, THIS IS JESUS THE KING OF THE JEWS. Then were there two thieves crucified with him, one on the right hand, and another on the left. And they that passed by reviled him, wagging their heads, And saying, Thou that destroyest the temple, and buildest it in three days, save thyself. If thou be the Son of God, come down from the cross. Likewise also the chief priests mocking him, with the scribes and elders, said, He saved others; himself he cannot save. If he be the King of Israel, let him now come down from the cross, and we will believe him. He trusted in God; let him deliver him now, if he will have him: for he said, I am the Son of God. The thieves also, which were crucified with him, cast the same in his teeth. Now from the sixth hour there was darkness over all the land unto the ninth hour. And about the ninth hour Jesus cried with a loud voice, saying, Eli, Eli, lama sabachthani? that is to say, My God, my God, why hast thou forsaken me? Some of them that stood there, when they heard that, said, This man calleth for Elias. And straightway one of them ran, and took a spunge, and filled it with vinegar, and put it on a reed, and gave him to drink. The rest *said, Let be, let us see whether Elias will come to save him. Jesus, when he had cried again with a loud voice, yielded up the ghost. And, behold, the veil of the temple was rent in twain from the top to the bottom; and the earth did quake, and the rocks rent; And the graves were opened; and many bodies of the saints which slept arose, And came out of the graves after his resurrection, and went into the holy city, and appeared unto many. Now when the centurion, and they that were with him, watching Jesus, saw the earthquake, and those things that were done, they feared greatly, saying, Truly this was the Son of God. And many women were there beholding afar off, which followed Jesus from Galilee, ministering unto him: Among which was Mary Magdalene, and Mary the mother of James and Joses, and the mother of Zebedee's children. When the even was come, there came a rich man of Arimathaea, named Joseph, who also himself was Jesus' disciple: He went to Pilate, and begged the body of Jesus. Then Pilate commanded the body to be delivered. And when Joseph had taken the body, he wrapped it in a clean linen cloth, And laid it in his own new tomb, which he had hewn out in the rock: and he rolled a great stone to the door of the sepulchre, and departed. And there was Mary Magdalene, and the other Mary, sitting over against the sepulchre. Now the next day, that followed the day of the preparation, the chief priests and Pharisees came together unto Pilate, Saying, Sir, we remember that that deceiver said, while he was yet alive, After three days I will rise again. Command therefore that the sepulchre be made sure until the third day, lest his disciples come by night, and steal him away, and say unto the people, He is risen from the dead: so the last error shall be worse than the first. Pilate said unto them, Ye have a watch: go your way, make it as sure as ye can. So they went, and made the sepulchre sure, sealing the stone, and setting a watch."*

MATTHEW CHAPTER TWENTY-SEVEN
"THOU SAYEST"

WORD OF FAITH SCRIPTURES FOR MEDITATION:
Matthew 27:11-14

> "And Jesus stood before the governor: and the governor asked him, saying, Art thou the King of the Jews? And Jesus said unto him, Thou sayest. And when he was accused of the chief priests and elders, he answered nothing. Then said Pilate unto him, Hearest thou not how many things they witness against thee? And he answered him to never a word; insomuch that the governor marvelled greatly."

WORD OF GOD MESSAGE FOR APPLICATION:

Jesus stands before the governor and being asked by the governor if He is King of the Jews? I wondered why Jesus did not let them know He was not only the King of the Jews, He was born a King. His kingdom was not of this world. He is King of kings and Lord of lords.

Jesus taught many lessons by His example. He is teaching us how we should respond when we are falsely accused by people you are trying to help. Jesus came into the world to save sinners and bring all who would believe and receive back to God.

Those whom Jesus came to redeem are falsely accusing Him. When you are falsely accused and you are brought before those who have power to sentence you, do as Jesus did; answer them not a word. When Jesus did not try to prove He was innocent, He confused His accusers. Pilate said to Jesus in Matthew 27:13, "Then said Pilate unto him, Hearest thou not how many things they witness against thee?"

Throughout life, you will find yourself in situations that will cause you humiliation, hurt and embarrassment. If the Lord does not give you the words to say, keep your mouth closed. You can keep your mouth shut, but never close the door to silent prayer. Jesus prayed in Matthew 26:36 for strength to suffer the shame of the cross. Jesus endured the cross and Jesus despised the shame.

Jesus took on our suffering, pain and shame so that we can suffer without fear. You must have faith in God and you must believe God is with you. Knowing God is with you might not stop the mouths of the false accusers and criticizers, but it will give you peace in the midst of your pain.

Here in chapter twenty-seven Jesus is asking God, "If it be possible let this cup pass. But I do not want My will to be fulfilled, I must fulfill the will of the Father." That should be your attitude also. Prayer is a powerful weapon. When you pray for those who mistreat you, God will give you great recompense of reward.

There is a process in the midst of pain. You don't hear teaching pertaining to the process and punishment as you go through the pain. During the process of pain, you must remember God is with you and through prayer and faith in the Word of God; the process of pain will empower you with the anointing.

Jesus' process began when they stripped Him, but they could not shake His security of the Father's care. They mocked Jesus, but they could not make Him doubt God. They spat on Him, but they could not separate Him from the love of God. The process of pain was bringing you to the place of peace and the power of God.

The process pressed Jesus into the place of power; power to prevail over death, hell and the grave. The process of your pain will lead you into the place of victory, peace and power. After the process and the test, you are ready to fulfill the will of God. You might feel forgotten and forsaken by God, but your day of resurrection will come. Jesus was crucified. He did die on the cross. They put His body in a tomb and Pilate put a watch over the tomb.

The last Scripture reads, "So they went, and made the sepulchre sure, sealing the stone, and setting a watch." (Matthew 27:66)

MATTHEW CHAPTER TWENTY-SEVEN
QUESTIONS FOR APPLICATION

1. Who took counsel against Jesus to put Him to death?
_____

2. Who was Jesus delivered to? _____

3. Who betrayed Jesus? _____

4. When Jesus was quest by the governor, what was His response?
_____
_____

NOTE: Jesus is demonstrating to you what your response should be when you are falsely accused. In Matthew 27:12, Matthew wrote, "And when he was accused of the chief priests and elders, he answered nothing." You don't need to answer every accusation that comes against you.

5. In the ninth hour, what was Jesus' cry? _____
_____

6. What happened to the veil in the temple when Jesus died? _____
_____

7. Who is the person the people wanted the governor to release?
_____

8. What did the Centurion and they that were with him say after the grave was opened? _____
_____

9. What did Jesus say He was going to do after three days? _____
_____

10. Why did the priests and the Pharisees come to Pilate and command

the sepulcher of Jesus be sealed? _____
_____
_____

MATTHEW CHAPTER TWENTY-EIGHT

"In the end of the sabbath, as it began to dawn toward the first day of the week, came Mary Magdalene and the other Mary to see the sepulchre. And, behold, there was a great earthquake: for the angel of the Lord descended from heaven, and came and rolled back the stone from the door, and sat upon it. His countenance was like lightning, and his raiment white as snow: And for fear of him the keepers did shake, and became as dead men. And the angel answered and said unto the women, Fear not ye: for I know that ye seek Jesus, which was crucified. He is not here: for he is risen, as he said. Come, see the place where the Lord lay. And go quickly, and tell his disciples that he is risen from the dead; and, behold, he goeth before you into Galilee; there shall ye see him: lo, I have told you. And they departed quickly from the sepulchre with fear and great joy; and did run to bring his disciples word. And as they went to tell his disciples, behold, Jesus met them, saying, All hail. And they came and held him by the feet, and worshipped him. Then said Jesus unto them, Be not afraid: go tell my brethren that they go into Galilee, and there shall they see me. Now when they were going, behold, some of the watch came into the city, and shewed unto the chief priests all the things that were done. And when they were assembled with the elders, and had taken counsel, they gave large money unto the soldiers, Saying, Say ye, His disciples came by night, and stole him away while we slept. And if this come to the governor's ears, we will persuade him, and secure you. So they took the money, and did as they were taught: and this saying is commonly reported among the Jews until this day. Then the eleven disciples went away into Galilee, into a mountain where Jesus had appointed them. And when they saw him, they worshipped him: but some doubted. And Jesus came and spake unto them, saying, All power is given unto me in heaven and in earth. Go ye therefore, and teach all nations, baptizing them in the name of the Father, and of the Son, and of the Holy Ghost: Teaching them to observe all things whatsoever I have commanded you: and, lo, I am with you alway, even unto the end of the world. Amen."

MATTHEW CHAPTER TWENTY-EIGHT
"FEAR NOT YE: FOR I KNOW THAT YE SEEK JESUS"

WORD OF FAITH SCRIPTURES FOR MEDITATION:
Matthew 28:5-7

"And the angel answered and said unto the women, Fear not ye: for I know that ye seek Jesus, which was crucified. He is not here: for he is risen, as he said. Come, see the place where the Lord lay. And go quickly, and tell his disciples that he is risen from the dead; and, behold, he goeth before you into Galilee; there shall ye see him: lo, I have told you."

WORD OF GOD MESSAGE FOR APPLICATION:

You will find a command and a promise in these verses that will destroy all fear if you will seek Jesus. All you need is not only in Jesus, but all you need is Jesus. He is not dead, He is alive. The devil could not destroy Him. He is risen just like He said.

Then Jesus spoke in verse 10 and said, "…Be not afraid…" That is a command. After the command came a commission and a promise. Jesus gave the commission in Matthew 28:18-20, which reads…

"And Jesus came and spake unto them, saying, All power is given unto me in heaven and in earth. Go ye therefore, and teach all nations, baptizing them in the name of the Father, and of the Son, and of the Holy Ghost: Teaching them to observe all things whatsoever I have commanded you: and, lo, I am with you alway, even unto the end of the world. Amen."

The promise came with power from God to produce the will of God in the earth. As sons of God, we have been given power over all the power of the devil. You must pray and have faith in God. You must believe you are a joint-heir with Jesus Christ.

It is written in Galatians 4:1-7…
"Now I say, That the heir, as long as he is a child, differeth nothing

> *from a servant, though he be lord of all; But is under tutors and governors until the time appointed of the father. Even so we, when we were children, were in bondage under the elements of the world: But when the fulness of the time was come, God sent forth his Son, made of a woman, made under the law, To redeem them that were under the law, that we might receive the adoption of sons. And because ye are sons, God hath sent forth the Spirit of his Son into your hearts, crying, Abba, Father. Wherefore thou art no more a servant, but a son; and if a son, then an heir of God through Christ."*

By faith, you are no longer a child but a son of God. Now that you are a son, you are a joint-heir with Jesus Christ. This is according to Romans 8:14-17 which reads…

> *"For as many as are led by the Spirit of God, they are the sons of God. For ye have not received the spirit of bondage again to fear; but ye have received the Spirit of adoption, whereby we cry, Abba, Father. The Spirit itself beareth witness with our spirit, that we are the children of God: And if children, then heirs; heirs of God, and joint-heirs with Christ; if so be that we suffer with him, that we may be also glorified together."*

We are joint-heirs with Jesus Christ in peace, power, authority and all things pertaining to life and godliness. Jesus came in the fullness of time to redeem us and bring many sons into glory. The Apostle Paul wrote in Galatians 4:4-7…

> *"But when the fulness of the time was come, God sent forth his Son, made of a woman, made under the law, To redeem them that were under the law, that we might receive the adoption of sons. And because ye are sons, God hath sent forth the Spirit of his Son into your hearts, crying, Abba, Father. Wherefore thou art no more a servant, but a son; and if a son, then an heir of God through Christ."*

When Jesus rose from the dead, He demonstrated the power He had over every power and work of the devil. That same power dwells in us. It is written in Romans 8:11, which reads, "But if the Spirit of him that raised up Jesus from the dead dwell in you, he that raised up Christ from the dead shall also quicken your mortal bodies by his Spirit that dwelleth in you."

MATTHEW CHAPTER TWENTY-EIGHT
QUESTIONS FOR APPLICATION

1. Who came to the sepulchre on the Sabbath? _____
_____

2. Why did they come to the sepulchre? _____
_____

3. Who did they find at the sepulchre when they arrived? _____
_____

4. Who had fear? _____

5. Whom were they seeking? _____

6. What were they told to do when they left the sepulchre? _____
_____
_____

7. Who met them as they went to tell the disciples? _____
_____
_____

8. What did Jesus tell them to do once they had seen Him? _____
_____
_____

9. Why was money given to the soldiers? _____
_____

10. What was the great commission given by Jesus to every Christian young and old? _____
_____
_____
_____

CONCLUDING THOUGHT
"COME BOLDLY"

"Let us therefore come boldly unto the throne of grace, that we may obtain mercy, and find grace to help in time of need." (Hebrews 4:16)

God has commanded you to come boldly before the throne of grace that you might find grace in time of trouble. We are living in a trouble time, but we do not serve a trouble God. Our God has called, commanded, us to be strong in the Lord and in the power of His might. It is not if you pray, but it is when you pray. When you pray, come boldly before His throne.

When you come boldly, you are coming in faith knowing God is a God of His Word. He has given us His promises. I asked God one day, why did He give us His promises? He spoke in my heart and said, "Dorothy, I gave them My promises so that they will realize how much I love them and to let them know the things I have in stored for them. Tell My people they must remember My love for them and My desire is to bring them back to Me so that I can fulfill Genesis 1:26. I created them to be in My image and after My likeness. Yes, the first Adam failed; but the second Adam, My Son, Jesus Christ, demonstrated My presence, My power and My peace in a world of sickness, poverty, death and tribulation. Tell My children they are My sons and My daughters and I love them. Also, tell My children, I come in their presence when they pray. I am with them and I will never leave them and I will not forsake them. Tell My children, in nothing be terrified by the devil." Thank You, Father!

God's power and God's presence comes upon you when you pray. Keep in mind; it does not matter if you are in the outer court of prayer or the inner court of prayer, as long as you begin your day with prayer. There are intercessors God has raised up and called them out of the people to intercede in prayer. God's intercessors have been anointed and appointed by God to intercede in the outer court – which is a type and shadow of those who have received Jesus as Savior and Lord of their lies, but do not know how to war a good warfare in prayer.

These intercessors are appointed and anointed by God to be your watchman on the wall as they pray for you until you realize the power of the blood of Jesus and the power of God's Word. There in the outer court, the brazen lava filled with water is a type and shadow of the power of God's Word to wash and cleanse you as you learn to live like a Son of God.

You are not alone in your walk with God and your warfare with the devil. It is in the outer court of prayer God's intercessors war in the earth realm and also in the heavens. You are surrounded by the prayers of God's intercessors and also the angels of God.

Every day of your life, you must prepare yourself for warfare. You are not just a conqueror; you are more than a conqueror through Christ Jesus. You must learn to decree and declare the promises of God over your life and into your life as you begin your day with prayer.

God's Word will work if you will begin your day by working God's Word in prayer. You must know what God's Word has said about your situation before you can pray God's Word into the situation. When the disciples came to Jesus in Luke 11:1, they asked Him to teach them to pray. In Matthew chapter six, Jesus gives the pattern of prayer. When I say the pattern of prayer, all prayers should be prayed in faith believing God is your Father. He will answer you. Yes! God always answer every prayer either by saying, "yes", "no" or "wait." Prayer should be prayed in the name of Jesus.

You became a son of God and joint heir of Jesus Christ when you received Jesus as Savior of your life. You not only have access into the presence of God by the blood of Jesus applied to your life; but the name of Jesus is your power of attorney to receive the promises of God. You have a legal right to believe and receive all that God has promised you in the realm of the earth and also the promises waiting for you in heaven. The blessings God has for His children are eternal. They begin in the earth, but they do not stop there. I believe the Word of the Lord in 1 Corinthians 2:9-10 which reads…

> *"But as it is written, Eye hath not seen, nor ear heard, neither have entered into the heart of man, the things which God hath prepared for them that love him. But God hath revealed them unto us by his Spirit: for the Spirit searcheth all things, yea, the deep things of God."*

When you pray, the Spirit will search the deep things of God and give you the grace to face any situation that comes your way. God might not reveal to you the trap the devil has set for you, but God will not leave you without an intercessor who will be assigned to intercede for you.

When the Spirit searches the deep things of God during prayer, God will reveal many of those things to the intercessors who know how to pray beyond the outer court. The deep things of God are revealed in the inner court of prayer. It is in the inner court of prayer there is the bread of God's presence, which is a type and shadow of God's presence in His Word.

You will also find the candles of illumination, revelation and impartation of the Spirit. The Spirit of God is present to reveal the deep things of God. It is here God will begin to reveal to the intercessors their spiritual assignment in prayer. There will be times the spirit of the intercessor will make divine connections with the Spirit of God and begin to groan in the Spirit. God does not reveal to them what they are praying about or who they are praying for; all they know is that they are interceding with words that cannot be uttered.
It is written in Romans 8:26-27…

> *"Likewise the Spirit also helpeth our infirmities: for we know not what we should pray for as we ought: but the Spirit itself maketh intercession for us with groanings which cannot be uttered. And he that searcheth the hearts knoweth what is the mind of the Spirit, because he maketh intercession for the saints according to the will of God."*

After the groaning and the travailing in prayer by God's intercessors in the Holy Place (which is also called the inner court), God will remove the veil of His hand and send Holy Spirit to usher them into His glory. In the glory of God's presence, those intercessors who have travailed in prayer for others now receive the fullness of joy and pleasures forever more because the glory of God's presence surrounds them.

Now, I speak by the presence and power of God into and over the lives of every intercessor God has anointed and appointed to pray beyond your sacrifice, suffering and separated life. God is with you and He will cause the glory of His presence to rest upon you as you intercede in prayer. I will set a guard over your children to the third and fourth generation. You shall be called, the restorer of the breach, the repairer of the waste places. This shall be done through prayer and the ministry of My Word. Always remember I am with you and I will never fail you. "…Not by might, nor by power, but by my spirit, saith the LORD of hosts." (Zechariah 4:6b)

Thank You, Jesus. Thank You, Father God, in heaven. We shall awaken and "Pray without Ceasing."

I believe there is a wake-up call to pray. Pray in faith and in God's Word through the name of Jesus and the blood of the Lamb which is our weapon of mass destruction.

To fortify you with the Word of God, you will find part three of Matthew. In part three of Matthew to inspire you also to study the Word of God, you will find chapters 21-28. If you do not have Matthew part one and two, they are available. But it does not matter where you start with these studies, Holy Spirit will supply all that you need from this study.

Each study has CDs of each class taught in our Spirit and Life School of Discipleship, Ministry and Bible College. Information is available to you by calling our business office Monday-Thursday from 10:00 a.m. to 12:00 noon and also 1:30-5:30 p.m. at (910) 423-2999 or write:

Outreach for Jesus Church
3320 Teakwood Drive
Hope Mills, NC 28348

www.ingramcontent.com/pod-product-compliance
Lightning Source LLC
Chambersburg PA
CBHW020017050426
42450CB00005B/512